NEW VISION OF GLORY

NEW VISION OF GLORY

by

RICHARD HOLLOWAY

LONDON: A. R. MOWBRAY & CO. LTD.
NEW YORK: A CROSSROAD BOOK
THE SEABURY PRESS

Text set in Monotype Bembo, and printed in Great Britain at The Pitman Press, Bath.

ISBN 0 264 66042 0 (Mowbray)
ISBN 0-8164-0260-4 (Seabury)

First published 1974
by A. R. Mowbray & Co. Ltd.
The Alden Press, Osney Mead,
Oxford, OX2 0EG

and

The Seabury Press
815 Second Avenue
New York, N.Y. 10017

TO

ANN,

SARA

AND

MARK

CONTENTS

PART ONE

PART TWO

ACKNOWLEDGEMENTS

The most difficult part of writing a book, I have discovered, is finding the right title. This volume has been called by a friend, 'the book of many titles', and with good reason. The fifth and final title was suggested by Richard Mulkern and William Purcell and I am very grateful to them—though I still have a soft spot for some of the rejected versions! William Purcell helped with more than the title. He read the book chapter by chapter as it was written, and provided much valuable advice and encouragement. I am most grateful to him. I must also thank Robert Nye for reading the whole manuscript and suggesting several valuable corrections. I am also extremely grateful to Richard Mulkern for his unfailing patience and helpfulness in the production side of the book. And I must also acknowledge my gratitude to my two colleagues, Martin Shaw and David Boag, for their great tact and patience in working with a rector who is frequently glued to the typewriter.

Part of chapter ten appeared originally as an article in the *Church Times*. I am most grateful to the editor for allowing me to use it again.

Extracts from *The Making of a Counter Culture* are reprinted by permission of Faber and Faber Ltd., and Doubleday, New York. Permission to quote from the *Jerusalem Bible* has been granted by Darton, Longman and Todd Ltd.

Mock on, mock on, Voltaire, Rousseau;
Mock on, mock on; 'tis all in vain!
You throw the sand against the wind,
And the wind blows it back again.

And every sand becomes a gem
Reflected in the beams divine;
Blown back they blind the mocking eye,
But still in Israel's paths they shine.

The atoms of Democritus
And Newton's particles of light
Are sands upon the Red Sea shore,
Where Israel's tents do shine so bright.

William Blake

PART ONE

1

The Word

ONE OF the most exhilarating and frustrating things about religion is the impossibility of ever being able to say the last word, of reaching an indisputable finality. No matter how confident a man is as to the firmness of his statement of religious fact, somewhere someone is lurking who will dispute it in every detail or in most. And of course there are those who believe that the effort to say *anything* about religion is wasted, since there is no reality behind the language, no correspondence in fact between what is said and what is actually *there*. One does not have to be an atheist or a logical positivist to allow a great deal of truth to this point of view: language *is* our problem. The problem arises because of the nature of language, of *talk*, of words. Language is a bit like the money system—if it is to be of use as a system there must be agreement between those who use it as a means of exchange as to the precise value of the symbols used. Money is a convenient device which operates upon the basis of agreed value. In itself, money is nothing; it is a symbol or token of no objective value which stands in for something else which is supposed to have value. This is quite obvious in the case of paper money which is an arbitrary means for conveying real value in convenient form. Even in the case of gold the value is purely subjective. We live in a culture which values gold, so gold is valuable in our culture. It is true that gold in itself is of more intrinsic worth than, say, paper, but it receives its worth from us and its worth is entirely related to our desires. There is an inevitable circularity about it all. In a real life-or-death situation the entirely arbitrary nature of 'value' is soon demonstrated. A man dying of thirst in the desert with a ton of gold in his land-rover would trade it all for a gallon of water, because in his particular predicament water is infinitely more valuable than gold. So money, in whatever form, is simply an agreed form of exchange which represents real things. And it can be used in most normal situations with a fair amount of certainty. It represents things like loaves and houses and cars and shoes, and can usually be exchanged for them. It is an agreed system of symbols representing certain hard realities. It is an exchange, an interchange of value, a mediating system. It works only because it is acceptable to those who use it. Occasionally it fails, as anyone who has ever tried to buy a ticket to the cinema in London with a Scottish pound note will testify. But this is only because there is disagreement as to the accepted value of the symbol. Once this is re-established the interchange continues. In the case of the London cinema, the outraged Scot simply sends for the manager who explains to the girl in the ticket-office that the Scottish pound note is an acceptable token of value, and the transaction continues.

On its most basic level, language is a similar system of exchange. A language is a simple system of exchange within a group, by means of which certain vocal symbols are accepted as representing real things. At its most basic level it serves as a convenient method of co-operation in joint ventures, such as eating at a large table with many people. The monosyllable 'salt' is an accepted verbal representation of the white stuff down at the other end of the table. According to the *Tarzan* method of communication, the simple enunciation of this single syllable, possibly reinforced by a corresponding gesture, is sufficient to suggest the meaning which is being conveyed; and the salt is duly passed down the table. Where a vocal interchange is impossible, as among Trappist monks and deaf-mutes, the interchange is conducted by means of hand-signals, and the same end is achieved.

Language, at this level, is a simple interchange because the meanings conveyed are fairly basic and tangible. As the philosophers put it, the symbols can be empirically verified without too much trouble. At this level there ought to be complete success in the communication of meaning, provided the participants speak the same language. It is often claimed that this basic use of language lays down certain definitive ground-rules for evaluating all language, no matter how abstract the matter which is being communicated. If, therefore, the verification system, the method relating symbol to the reality which it symbolises, is complex and disputable, it has sometimes been held that nothing of any meaning is being conveyed. The most obvious example is the use of the monosyllable *God*. It is held by some that this is a vocal symbol which represents a reality or Reality itself. But it is obvious that *God* cannot be verified as simply as the salt at the end of the table. Thus it has been claimed that the word *God* has no ascertainable meaning and cannot be held to convey information about reality.

The same blissfully simple method can be applied to all religious language, with devastating effect. If the *Tarzan* verification method is adopted, it destroys the possibility of communicating objective reality by means of religious language and symbol, since the reality behind the symbolism is clearly not verifiable by this method. And there is no doubt that the *Tarzan* method has influenced a great deal of writing and thinking on the subject of religion in recent years. Where the method is taken over as valid, it has interesting effects on religious language.[1] If religious language is held to be subject to this simple test, then its meaning must be transposed if it is to continue in use. It must be made to apply to something which *can* be verified by this method. The most common transposition is in the direction of what we might call a *morality-fortifying myth.* The religious symbol or narrative is held to be a rather complex device for *describing* and *enabling* the moral convictions held by the subject (presumably on other grounds, verified in an appropriate way).

But even in this apparently logical resolution of the problem there are two pitfalls. First of all, it is never exactly or satisfactorily explained why the religious symbol, now voided of objective content, is held to *enable* as well as describe the chosen moral attitude. This is particularly noticeable in the use of the words and example of Jesus to achieve this kind of end. These are held to illuminate the moral dilemmas of man by a strange attractive power which is, apparently, inherent in Jesus himself. But the power and attractiveness of Jesus does not seem to be subject to the verification method used to validate the other symbols. His compelling power must be intrinsic and irreducible; in other words, a clear departure from the method. His power can only be explained by some sort of hidden assumption or disguised metaphysic. This apparent break in the method is related to the second pitfall. It does not seem possible to provide a sufficiently compelling authority for *any* moral attitude simply by an analysis of the language used to describe it. A moral attitude implies a sense of responsibility which *catches* the subject and lays an obligation upon him. And the obligation he feels cannot be reduced to any other terms than itself. It has an intrinsic and undeniable power, an immovable objectivity which cannot be avoided. This sense of moral obligation is very clear in many of the theologians who have reduced theology to the status of *morality-fortifying myth.* It is particularly clear, for instance, in the writings of Alistair Kee and other Christian radicals, who are driven by a sense of overwhelming obligation to the oppressed and under-privileged. It is significant that the reasons why Jesus should be accepted as the authoritative source of this taxing moral attitude are never clearly stated; they are simply taken for granted as self-evident. This is clearly a break in the verification principle upon which the whole enterprise is based.

Clearly, this resolution of the problem of religious language raises enormous difficulties. It seems unlikely that it will commend itself to any who are not already Christian, though it is proclaimed with almost evangelical passion by those who hold to it as being the only way in which modern man can use the Christian tradition. There has, however, been no significant growth in the numbers of those who follow this way. Its main appeal is to those who are still within the Christian tradition, yet find their position an uneasy and perplexing one. They are unable to shake themselves completely free of a faith which seems no longer tenable yet continues to exert an inexplicable power over them. There can be little doubt that this is the only way in which many within the Christian tradition can 'believe' today, but it is too complex and intellectual a way to have any but a sectional appeal. F. D. Maurice once said that men were usually right in what they affirmed and wrong in what they denied. If those who hold to this way would only affirm it as that part of the continent of faith where they still have a foothold, without going on to refute the existence of a vaster hinterland, then their position would be viewed with more sympathy. It is a mean-spirited explorer who chooses to remain on the beach of a mysterious island, yet scoffs at those who are half way up the cliffs or on into the woods beyond.

Fortunately, the admitted difficulties of religious language need not leave Faith on that dismal beach. It is commonly recognised today that there are various levels or types of language, and that the raw application of the simple verification technique is not the only method of dealing with them. Language can become an elusive and complicated thing, but this is often because the realities it is meant to convey are themselves difficult to grasp. This elaboration of the status of language allows religious language a role. It is used within the group who claim to have experienced the reality the language is meant to convey. Within the religious group, the language has an accepted value, an accepted meaning. It is a genuine currency within that group.

But this does not get us very far in discovering whether or not there is any reality behind the language. The paper money used in a game of Monopoly could be held to be a genuine currency among those playing the game, but it is also recognised that it has no objective value apart from the game; it is an imitation currency in any other context. Is this the sense in which religious language is a language? Is it simply an imitation language, with no reality behind it, a concessionary language for those who like to play the game called Faith? We are in real difficulties here. In all the language groups to which religious thinkers point as analogous, there is something behind the language which *you can get at*. In the language of poetry or the emotions, there is usually some analysable object which can be pointed to as being, somehow, the *stimulus* behind the symbol.

In the case of religious language, however, we continue to draw a blank. There are lots of *experiences* to which we can point, and from which data can be built up, but we cannot seem to get at that which is experienced. We cannot verify God. He is always off stage, the hidden God. This need not distress the believer too much, though it is clearly a frustration, but it is a frustration which is unavoidably built in to the religious experience itself. By his very nature, God is that which cannot be communicated or verified by any other method of verification than that which is appropriate to his own nature. And this is where the man of faith experiences his most acute frustration, and, for some, their most acute crisis of belief. When he is asked to 'verify' what he is talking about when he talks about God, when he is asked to unpack his language, lay, as it were, the symbol alongside the reality which it represents, he is faced with an impossibility. If he seems to succeed in doing what is requested he, in fact, fails most completely, because what he has verified cannot be God! Every other model of verification is inappropriate and nullifying if applied to the language of Faith, because they are all based, in one way or another, on data which are available to our senses, and God is not available to our senses *in that way*. 'And if anyone, when he has seen God, understands what he has seen, it is never God that he has seen, but some one of those things of His which exist and are known.'[2]

> There is none other God but He that none may know, which may not be known. No, soothly, no! Without fail, No, says she. He only is my God that none can one word of say, nor all they of Paradise one only point attain nor understand, for all the knowing that they have of him.[3]

This is why in one ancient theological tradition God is defined only in negatives. An almost liturgical responsory is built up in which a statement of man's attempt to define God is laid out and immediately denied, 'yet this is not God'. This is sometimes called the way of 'the rejection of images', in which the central and sustaining conviction is that the Absolute cannot be stated in relative terms, and since only relative terms are available to us, he cannot be stated at all.

In other words, the language of Faith cannot be translated into any other language without a profound denial of its meaning. Translation is, in fact, assassination or, as it has been called, 'the death of a thousand qualifications'. There seems to be a great gulf fixed, so that 'they which would pass from hence to us cannot, neither can we pass to them'. And this gulf is the greatest temptation and frustration experienced by the man of Faith who would give an account of the Faith that is in him. If he embarks upon the language-game with the unbeliever, he finds himself travelling down a one-way street. And many have gone that way and have found no means of returning whence they came. Others have simply positioned themselves on the opposite bank of the gulf and have offered up the liturgy of their faith in a defiant vernacular which cares not whether the world hears or whether it forbears.

This is far from being a satisfactory situation, and few Christians have been able to sustain it for long. There have been a number of attempted solutions, most of them on a briskly practical level, because the practical Christian is usually convinced anyway that there is no way of arguing people into faith, and he is usually impatient with what he thinks is excessive reliance upon formal and technical discussions of religion. Such a man will maintain that the only successful verification or authentication of religion is the life of the man of faith. 'By their fruits ye shall know them.' Good works and a holy life are the only effective argument for faith. They are the effects of which true religion is the cause. The examplary lives of the Faithful cause men to enquire as to the source of such virtue and power. They are attracted to the Faith, not as an intellectual system or account of reality, but simply as a way of life. They see lives being healed and cleansed, and they are challenged, on a practical level, to try it for themselves. Faith, therefore, is caught, not taught.

Now there is undoubtedly a great deal in this point of view, and many notable conversions have been occasioned by exposure to such infectious holiness. The proper integrity of Faith requires a response throughout every aspect of a man's life. Holiness *is* undoubtedly a powerful missionary force. Nevertheless there are enormous difficulties in leaving the matter just like that.

The first difficulty is the most obvious. Christians do not have a corner in the holiness-market. If all good and holy lives were Christian lives, there would be enormous persuasive power in that fact. But it is certainly not the case.

Goodness is not just a Christian phenomenon. There have been saints, men and women who have led lives of conspicuous holiness and dedication, in all religions and among those who have no religion. Even if it could be demonstrated that there have been more of them in the Church than out, the fact that any have been able to achieve sanctity from outside the tradition means that the tradition cannot be pointed to as the sole determining factor. And most men know this. The facts are too various to permit of a single connecting cause. And, anyway, if good works can '*verify*' the Faith logic demands that evil works ought to *falsify* it, and the Christian record is just as open to the latter interpretation as to the former.

A more weighty objection lies in the simple scarcity value of holiness! The fact is that Christians are not conspicuously better than non-Christians. The expectation that they ought to be is a result of the moralising of religion which has been so marked a characteristic of Western Christianity for centuries. Christians know no short-cut to goodness, though they ought to know a good deal about the profound reality of forgiveness. The Christian Gospel is first and foremost about what God is like and has done for man. Western Christianity has inverted the order, and produced a moralistic religion with most of its emphasis upon what man can do for God or his fellows. The very word *Christian* has changed its meaning. It is no longer used as a morally neutral term which defines a man's religious status. Instead, it has become a value term which describes a man's goodness. The fact that today Christianity is more likely to be defined in the language of social and political morality, rather than in the language of personal morality preferred by an earlier generation, does not alter the main fact. Christianity has become moralistic. There is some evidence to show that this is a peculiarly British heresy, and it is perhaps no accident that Pelagius was British. Maybe we ought to learn something from the Russian nobleman in Rebecca West's *The Birds Fall Down:*

> ... the piety of the English is a mockery. They want a prescription for social order and union with God means nothing to them. So they pretend that this is what religion is for: to teach men and women to be moral. But we Russians know that religion is for the moral and the immoral. It is the love of God for man meeting with the love of man for God, and God loves the vicious and the criminal and the idle as well as He loves the industrious and the honest and the truthful and the abstinent. He humbles himself to ask for the love of the murderer, the drunkard, the liar, the beggar, the thief. Only God can achieve this sublime and insane relationship.[4]

The fact is that Christians come to the search for goodness with as many private handicaps and inhibitions as their Marxist and humanist friends, and with no better results. It is for this reason that there can be no simple identikit picture of the Christian. We are all in different stages and different places. For some men the achievement of moderate virtue is the result of a degree of struggle that would have produced an apparently sanctified personality in a less complex subject. It is wiser not to judge another man's goodness, and it is foolish to bother too much about your own, even if it is in the cause of winning souls for Christ.

But the profoundest objection to this doctrine of verification of Faith by good works is that it also destroys the Faith it is claiming to justify. It is simply another, if subtler, method of assassination. This can be shown immediately on a purely logical level, though the main criticism must be theological. First of all, we must remember that a verification process involves something like the equalising of the symbol to be verified with the object it represents. In the case of the word *salt* the logic is obvious: *salt* is that white stuff at the end of the table, and that white stuff at the end of the table is *salt*. We have a useful test of reversibility which we can apply. When we apply it to 'the good works verifies Faith doctrine', we get startling results. If it is a genuine verification test, then the principle of reversibility must apply. Let's try it and see where we land.

The doctrine is, remember, that a man's Faith is verified by his goodness, or holiness, in short, his *works*. Faith must, somehow, be equalised with good conduct if it is to be verified by it. And when we apply the test of reversibility we come up with the answer that *works is Faith*. In other words, Faith is simply Morals, which is the same old song set to a slightly different tune, but no more acceptable than it was before; in fact less acceptable, because here we are dealing with a subtle deception. Those theologians who have reduced Faith to Morals are usually quite frank about what they are up to; they don't ambush us from behind just when we think we're getting somewhere. They show us quite frankly which garden path they are leading us up, and we can, if we are wise, politely refuse to follow them.

But the practical man of Faith has led us thence by a more devious route, and we're still miles off the King's highway! No matter what you call it or how you do it, if Faith is verified in this way it ceases to be Faith and becomes yet another human activity, and an activity of peculiar sadness. It leaves the whole burden of the Faith upon shoulders that cannot bear it; it demands from men a response which they are constitutionally incapable of making. If Faith can only be 'verified' in the eyes of men by our actions, then we are of all men most miserable, for which of us does not stand condemned every day of lovelessness and failure? Which of us is not smudged and stained by regret and compromise and headlong flight from responsibility? No man is able to bear this weight, and there is a desperate pride in trying to bear it because it negates the gracious action of God in Christ. This ancient and apparently endless debate is the heart of the message of the Apostle Paul.

> I am not annulling God's grace; no, but if saving righteousness comes by way of the law, then indeed Christ's death was useless.
>
> You are for justification by the law [we could easily read, *verification by works*]? Then you have done with Christ, you have deserted grace, for it is by faith that we wait in the Spirit for the righteousness we hope for. Gal. 2.21; 5.4ff.

And here we are very close to the heart of the Gospel itself. Paul's main theme, trumpeted again and again throughout his ministry, is this: Why did God make all that fuss in Christ if men were capable of the kind of righteousness or good works which are demanded of them? Because the claim made by the Gospel in Paul and in parable after parable in the Synoptists is that God loves us and justifies us *in our sins, in spite of our sins, and through and over and under our sins.* Our tragedy is precisely that we have *no* righteousness, that we are caught in a desperate trap of moral powerlessness, searching for a goodness we cannot arrive at on our own, 'for all have sinned and come short of the glory of God' (Rom. 3.23).

This fact of human alienation and extremity is the glorious opportunity grasped by God. So amazing did his love seem to the old poets of the Church that they called the sin of man a *happy fault*, *felix culpa*, because it provided the context for the overwhelming graciousness of God who loved us 'while we were yet sinners'. The Gospel begins and ends and is always and endlessly repeated round this theme of the gracious and continuing initiative of God in Christ who 'loved us and gave himself for us'. This is the primary and abiding fact of the Christian Gospel. It is this which justifies 'the vicious and the criminal and the idle, as well as the industrious and the honest and the truthful and the abstinent'; *and* the racist and the revolutionary, the neo-Marxist and the chairman of the Monday Club, the editor of *Oz* and the man who writes the leaders for the *Daily Telegraph*. The old Russian was right, only God could achieve such a 'sublime and insane relationship'.

So sublime and insane is the primary fact of the Christian Gospel that it has been an offence to men in every generation, not least to those who have called themselves Christians. Men are for ever trying to make the Gospel a little more logical, give it a little more justice, make it a bit more acceptable to the fastidiously democratic sensibility of modern, liberal man. But it won't work, in spite of the avid rhetoric of our modern Pelagians. The Gospel is an offence, a piece of divine idiocy that only God could get away with. Only he would dare offer the same wages to those who have laboured but one hour as to those who have laboured all day or have laboured not at all. Central to the Message is the impelling and releasing fact that men are not able of themselves to help themselves, but that they have a Helper who has created and sustained them and who adds grace upon grace by saving them 'while they are yet in their sins,' without condition and without reproach. This is the promise, the certainty which has burned within the Christian tradition for 2000 years. And how can we now validate and verify this Faith to a world which needs it, by basing our method upon a premise that contradicts it in every way? To offer men Morals when they need Salvation is to offer them stones for bread, and to add the further injury of describing the stone as a whole-wheat loaf. Better to do nothing than to do that!

The method of practical verification gets us no further than the other efforts at mistranslation. Is this the end of it, then? Is there no way in which the man of Faith can build a bridge between his experience and the experience of the unbeliever, the searcher, the doubter? Are we destined to remain a world of strangers, confused by a multitude of tongues? Or is there some unity of meaning which transcends our differences, where the dialogue can be renewed in a different way?

Before we can go any further we must shift our ground. When an engineer builds a bridge across a gulf he has to make sure there is solid ground on either side to receive it. You can't build a bridge on a swamp and you can't build a bridge between Faith and Unbelief on the swamp of linguistics. And the nature of language should have warned us of this. Language is nothing unless it relates to shared experience, accepted realities, and even at its best it is a fragile method of exchange. Life is tragically full of examples of man's inability to communicate the fullness of his heart to his neighbour. The very words which should bridge the loneliness between us frequently widen the gulf and become weapons which deepen the hatred and incomprehension. By some mysterious chemistry of sin, the very means of exchange, the mediating symbols, become barriers to our unity. The cynical practitioner of *real-politik* can manipulate language to darken and confuse the truth; the advertising copywriter can debase and devalue a whole vocabulary to suit his own ends; politicians dissemble, and lovers deceive; even the innocent and well-intending find themselves trapped by words in weird predicaments—and all use the same fragile interchange. Language is an apt parable of our strange condition. It mocks us with borrowed laughter. None of this should come as any surprise to the Christian, for he ought to know what is in man. Yet, for some strange reason, we often seem to exclude the intellect from the consequences of what Christian tradition calls the Fall of Man. This is the one Christian doctrine for which there is no lack of empirical verification! There is in man a profound distortion at the very centre of his being which affects everything he does, and nothing is protected from its infection. His closest and most sacred relationships are affected, and his very understanding of his own nature is clouded and confused because of it. It has sometimes been called man's Original Sin, in the sense that it is radically entrenched within his own being. It normally expresses itself in a conviction as to the centrality of his own selfhood. It is man's inalienable tragedy. His manhood is a fallen manhood, and his words are fallen and flawed by the same taint. If, then, words are of dubious value in man's dealings with his own kind, how can we be surprised that they fail so completely to mediate the Otherness of God?

But we are in a deeper predicament even than that which is caused by the ambiguity of our words. The man of Faith is dealing with an experience of such power and strangeness that it defeats even his *truest* efforts to express and contain it. He is like the artist who has to express a three-dimensional reality on a flat, two-dimensional surface. The artist does it by *suggesting* depth through the device of perspective, thereby conveying truth by deception. All art is a struggle to communicate reality by symbol. Yet, since the symbols are always inadequate to the reality they seek to convey, artists are always 'deceivers, yet true'. Our predicament is much more terrifying. Heaven and the heaven of heavens cannot contain him, how much less the frail symbols of human language! How on earth can we mediate *anything* of the mystery of God in *words*, those tired and inflated tokens of exchange?

Liberation from this tyrannous urge to convince others comes to the man of Faith at the moment he realises that *he cannot*, and need not try. He has plenty of work to do, but he is not called upon to do what is only possible for God, and *only* God can reveal himself. This brings us near the clue to the whole predicament. The man of Faith is not dealing with data which are mysteriously unavailable to the atheist. He does not have access to a country from which others are excluded and of whose existence he must persuade them by detailed descriptions of what he has seen there. He is not expected to know the habits of the purple unicorn. The man of Faith does not see different things; he sees the same things differently. Faith does not consist in *what* is seen but in the *way* of seeing. It is the same world which is made available to the senses of all men, but Faith sees it in a strange and luminous depth, and this seeing is something which comes as a gift.

The world presents itself as revelation, as bearing a grandeur and meaning to which adoration is the only appropriate response. The nearest analogous experience is falling in love. Charles Williams was one of the few theologians who saw the profound theological significance of romantic love. The experience of romantic love is certainly the closest model of that state of vision we call Faith. When a man falls in love he finds himself, according to Williams, 'by a process utterly beyond his own will, in a state of adoration'. Suddenly his beloved is charged with a significance and glory which is not at all apparent to those unfortunate enough not to behold her as he does. The most commonplace gesture of an apparently commonplace person becomes loaded with a beauty and meaning that is at once joyous and heart-breaking. And this state affects the lover's whole attitude towards the world. Dante describes how, when he saw Beatrice, if anyone had done him an injury, he could not but have forgiven it.

> This is perhaps the cardinal point. It does not mean a vague goodwill towards Chinamen, but a definite humility towards one's neighbour. Humility is bestowed in that state of adoration; the lover—it is the cliché of sentimentality—feels unworthy. Of course he does, he is, and Romantic Love is a state of facts.[5]

Williams maintained that this state of fleeting awareness is not abnormal; it is the true way of seeing things. It is a genuine illumination of the way things really are. It is man's tragedy as believer and lover that the vision is fleeting and difficult to sustain, but it is the authentic way of seeing, and it does allow a glimpse of the real significance of things. The problem has always lain in maintaining an obedience to the original vision, and preserving the conviction of its reality against the taunts of the cynical and myopic. Only a lover can understand a lover, and Faith can only speak to Faith. Language is an agony for both lover and believer, since each feels compelled to interpret and express the inexpressible. This accounts for the extraordinary banality of lovers and believers in seeking to describe their vision. If we fix our attention upon their language alone then we only achieve a state of mutual exasperation. To understand the lover or the man of Faith you have to learn to see as he sees, to experience what he experiences. And it is this fact which gives the believer his liveliest optimism. C. S. Lewis said somewhere that the world was a very dangerous place for the conscientious atheist, and that he couldn't be too careful as he made his way about it. There is no way of knowing when the vision will blaze out and capture the unwary or surprise him with a joy he had not sought. The facts are there, 'God himself has made it plain—for ever since the world was created, his invisible nature, his everlasting power and divine being, have been quite perceptible in what he has made' (Rom. 1.20). *We* do not provide the data of Faith, but we may be able to help others to see. The only place where the bridge can be built between Faith and Unbelief is at the place of patient waiting.

But there is a dark side to the vision. The kind of seeing which we call Faith is like those old optical illusions, which suddenly and fleetingly give a sense of depth to the flatness and allow us to see an added dimension. But the flatness *is* flatness and it, too, is part of the mystery. The man of Faith must not pretend to himself or to others that there is not also a darker way of seeing and that it too is there. To see through the universe to the glory behind it, we must look *at* the universe, and admit that there is a kind of seeing which we call despair. The vision is given and we cannot command it; the despair, too, may be the only honesty left to those to whom it has not been given. In other words, the experience of unbelief is a genuine experience and, like the experience of Faith, it is there before the arguments are mustered which support it. That is where we must begin to build the bridge.

2

The Protest

FAITH AND Unbelief are sisters; they are related ways of experiencing reality. Or, to use Professor Geddes McGregor's suggestive phrase, one is a descant upon the other. They are different ways of seeing the mystery of existence, different moods of awareness, but it is one mystery which is seen, though it shows itself now as fair, now as dark and impenetrable. The puzzle is one, though sometimes the patient watcher is rewarded by the glimpse of many dimensions, sometimes by nothing beyond an unyielding flatness. Faith and its dark sister Unbelief are primordial experiences, that is to say, they come before any attempt to explain or intellectualise them. The ability to intellectualise the primary experience or awareness is a very secondary affair, indulged in mainly by professional theorisers; and the original awareness has very little to do with cleverness. Indeed, the ability to talk and intellectualise may actually inhibit the ability to see and enjoy, or experience despair at patterns unseen.

There is something attenuated and impoverished about intellectual ability which has lost contact with the primitive ability simply to see and be aware. Our western culture is very clever, and very shallow and silly because of its cleverness. We seem to have cut off contact from our primordial response to reality, so we have produced a society which is neither joyful nor tragic, merely brash and jejune. We are like a photographer from one of the Sunday colour supplements doing a lay-out on Mount Sinai, who is too pleased with his own cleverness to be challenged by its awe-fulness. The photographer, in fact, is the very archetype of our modern technocratic culture. He distances himself from reality in order to record it in a medium that is flat and two-dimensional, and never really enters the mystery that is out there. The photographer must remain uninvolved, permanently detached, in order to follow his trade. It is not for him to enter the burning building, to penetrate the harrowing mystery, to risk himself. If he did that he might miss a good shot, a scoop. He is the complete observer, the camera eye, the aperture through which the surface of reality is filtered. This is not to say that the photographer shows no courage in the pursuit of his trade, but it is a courage which is carefully disciplined to his main purpose. Even if he is moved to comfort the stricken, to go to the rescue of the endangered, he must first catch the image of sorrow on those endless reels of celluloid which so typify our culture. The successful observer must, therefore, school himself against involvement with the mystery before him. He must learn to keep a psychic distance between himself and what confronts him, or his observer status will be compromised and his professionalism endangered.

But this is not the primary response to reality. Clinical detachment like this must be learnt. Man's *primary* relationship with reality is that of belonging and involvement. He is part of what he sees, and he feels it before he records or annotates it. He is *open* to what is out there, is connected to it by all sorts of links. Reality forces itself upon him, and it comes as Clarity or as Darkness, as Faith or Unbelief. The mystery of being reveals itself with joyful suddenness, or it remains tight shut against him. Man experiences reality in this primordial vision as either Meaning or Tragedy. It is not possible to say which is before or after the other, and for many men both are held in a strange tension.

Since Unbelief is a mood of awareness, it is best described in a personal and impressionistic way. This is why all the best descriptions of Unbelief are found in literature and rarely ever in systematic philosophical writing. Theoretical expositions of Unbelief are usually as gutless as their theological counterparts. The poet or novelist, on the other hand, enters into the mood of Unbelief so completely that we *feel* what he is talking about even before our minds find reasons for or against the experience. Real Unbelief, like real Faith, is not clinical and objective; it is passionately subjective, tortured by the darkness of its private vision. Like all great preaching, it is the cry of a dying man to dying men. The paradox and greatness of real Unbelief lies in its intensely moral awareness that something is not right with the universe. It is not the result of a calm and detached examination of reality, leading to a considered and well-documented conclusion. The true Unbeliever is *offended* by the universe; it outrages his sense of justice and pity. His Unbelief is a protest against the way things are. Like Dostoevsky's Ivan Karamazov he simply refuses to be a part of it. He returns the ticket, he won't co-operate. In what follows I have no intention of attempting to produce a systematic analysis of Unbelief. Instead, I want to enter the experience of Unbelief, to try to capture its mood of awareness. What I have to say is unashamedly subjective; it is my own Unbelief which I am describing; but I offer it because I am convinced that man is most universal when he is most like himself.

Unbelief, the inability to find meaning in reality, is one of the dominant moods of our culture. The modern experience of Unbelief is intensely related to the urban society man has created and which, increasingly, dictates and dominates his life. There is something about man's urban environment which darkens and confuses his sight and traps him in a spiritual isolation. To experience Unbelief at its most jagged and desolating one must begin in the City, and any city will do. New York City, however, is where I choose to begin, since it is the most dramatic example of Western man's urban culture; it is as much a symbol as it is a place.

Long before I ever visited New York its famous skyline was known to me from a hundred films and photographs. My copy of Dvorák's 'New World Symphony' came in a record-sleeve which bore a photograph of the tip of lower Manhattan at sunset, and I never think of Manhattan without hearing those poignant and thrilling opening bars. I go to any film which is made about New York in order to capture again that strange mixture of exaltation and desolation which this most fascinating of all cities holds for me. Something of this double mood is captured in the opening sequences of the film *West Side Story*. They are taken from a plane flying in to New York. The first glimpse you get is of that famous skyline at the tip of Manhattan. From the distance it looks majestic, with its weirdly ordered arrangement of massive buildings. As you come in closer you fly over the great avenues of skyscrapers, with strangely moving traffic far below. The mood is still one of order and peculiar grandeur.

There is no sound from the streets. But gradually the mood changes. The plane swoops lower, buildings take on meaning, and soon all you can see are rows of fire-escapes clinging like hideous insects to miles of peeling tenements. You are over the West Side, and you are aware of the sudden shift of meaning and mood. The poverty and squalor and desolation seem to rise in the air with suffocating intensity. You experience the city as tragedy. And both experiences are true, for New York is at once a fascinating and beautiful city and a concentration camp of appalling human misery: the glory and the shame, the promise and the squalid reality.

As you move about the streets and absorb their influence, an almost physical tightening of the heart occurs. There seems to be no pattern, no opening to the beyond, no exit. You are faced with millions of colliding and unrelated bodies, locked away inside themselves, 'living and partly living'. Sudden glimpses of empty eyes, gazing from the steps of fading brownstones; voices raised and stifled behind torn curtains; an overwhelming sense of muffled irritation; and the sense of hopeless waiting, like one of those junctions in the desert where the trains never stop any more. In the main streets the mood is different, more hectic and fevered, more desperate. Here the city offers its palliatives—the porn shops and the cinemas, the amusement parlours, the high and empty laughter, the heartbreaking swagger. And any city is the same. All perform the same dance; all know the same sudden explosions of violence and the same hectic search for an elusive happiness, for the City is one. Forty-second Street in New York and the High Street in Edinburgh are only separated by space and style—the experience is the same. Stop and ask the man on any side-walk in any city: he doesn't know and he'd rather not ask; he lives on the surface of a riddle that never reveals its meaning.

> Faces along the bar
> Cling to their average day:,
> The lights must never go out,
> The music must always play,
> All the conventions conspire
> To make this fort assume
> The furniture of home;
> Lest we should see where we are,
> Lost in a haunted wood,
> Children afraid of the night
> Who have never been happy or good.[1]

But the man on the High Street is not in the darkest place, for he at least buys dreams. Think of all the unknown men in all the unnumbered back streets in all the towns that ever were, and count the desperation and the blankness in all those eyes! The arithmetic of despair is unbelievable. All the cities that ever were and all their inhabitants add up to a weight of humanity whose very size renders it meaningless.[2] The suffocating fecundity of man! To take a train ride through the ravaged landscape of industrial Britain is to catch only the fringe of the experience: a jumbled kaleidoscope of gas-works and back streets and 'acres of dismantled cars'; faces fixed in doorways and drying-greens, cinema queues and factory gates; the faces of the unrecalled and unremarked, millions of faces.

> They watched the landscape, sitting side by side
> —An Odeon went past, a cooling tower,
> And someone running up to bowl—and none
> Thought of the others they would never meet
> Or how their lives would all contain this hour.[3]

And so it was in the back streets of Tyre and Sidon and Babylon and Rome, and so it is in Manchester and Glasgow and Chicago, Illinois. What can it all mean, this endless prodigality of being, this weight of longing and fear, these half-remembered hopes? 'Thick darkness covers the earth, and gross darkness the people.' To expose oneself to such unmitigated reality is to experience the shock of meaninglessness, of Unbelief; it is to break against a locked and uninterpreted universe; it is to know the dark and only the dark.

And it is in the darkness that man finds himself most vulnerable. He feels smaller at night. The feeling is best captured at three or four in the morning when you are driving through a strange town. You slow right down because of the speed limit, but mainly because, if you are like me, strange small towns in the middle of the night are fascinating. Even the harshest, ugliest town is strangely softened by the night, as sleep makes the plainest child lovely. So you slow down and almost crawl through the darkened, sleeping town. And before you reach the top of the hill and the end of the town, there's a light in a window. The only light in town. Someone awake in a town asleep. You're past the lighted window and out into the country again, and the light is still on. It could be a wakeful baby, fussed over by a new mother. Or someone suddenly ill. Or a sleepless old man poking the fire and looking into the past. One lighted window in a dark town. It creates a mild disturbance in the back of your mind as you cut your way through the night. And it's the darkness and the strange silence of a sleeping town and the yellow, unexpected light at the top of the street.

Or you are a priest called out in the middle of the night to someone who is dying, and you feel strangely vulnerable and crumpled as you walk through the darkened ward to the bed with the screens drawn round it. You perform the ritual of sealing a soul for death, while the ward is filled with the troubled breathing of the sick and the whole city sleeps. It creates a disturbance in the back of your mind as you return through the night. And again it's the darkness and the strange silence of a sleeping hospital, and the yellow, unexpected light over the bed at the top of the ward.

The night, though it has its beauty, is a bad time for men. The lost feel most lost at night. The despairing despair most. And most people die at night. It's as if a man's defences against all he fears most are weakened at night. Even the secure and the happy and the strong are at their lowest ebb, their most vulnerable, at night. And, of course, night is the time when evil rides out. Witches used to dance at night and body-snatchers snatched at night. In our century, the century of the secret police, the night is the time of the Arrest. In Hitler's Germany, the Jew would lie in bed at night waiting for the slamming of the car door in the street below, the pounding of feet on the stair, the smash of a shoulder against the door. Then the ride to a dreary building in the centre of town. It was the same in Stalin's Russia. It is the same in Vorster's South Africa. The night is congenial to this kind of thing. The secret police know their trade. They know that men find it difficult to be brave at night. That's why they come.

What is it about the night that disturbs us and causes us to drop our defences? It is because the night cuts us down to size. We are all good at pretending to ourselves that all is well. We ask no questions of life. We run from our loneliness. And we can do this during the day when the world is awake and conspires with us to muffle and suppress our unbidden doubts. But the doubts come back at night. At night you suddenly catch sight of yourself as a speck of dust on a small planet in a dark universe, surrounded by an emptiness that doesn't even echo. Is this man? Are we thrown from nothing into nothing? Is our life just this? Is there nothing from which we come, nothing towards which we go? Is our life just a tiny streak of light in the dark, a window aflame in a sleeping town? Are all the dead simply dead, and does our life end just like that—one moment a dancing flame and the next quenched for ever? This is the doubt that catches the heart as spaceship earth travels through the endless night: that out there is only thick darkness and an immensity of nothingness—and no God! Man is alone in the universe. To experience yourself as being Alone is Unbelief.

But, of course, Unbelief has its own compassion and humour and courage. It can produce a tenderness and tolerance towards all men caught, as they are, in the same predicament. It can cut a man's pretensions down to size by contrasting his small purposes with the immensity of meaninglessness that surrounds him. There is something of this quality in the opening piece in Harry Golden's *Only in America*, where he tells us why he never bawls out a waitress who has brought him the wrong order:

> I have a rule against registering complaints in a restaurant; because I know that there are at least four billion suns in the Milky Way—which is only one galaxy. Many of these suns are thousands of times larger than our own, and vast millions of them have whole planetary systems, including literally billions of satellites, and all of this revolves at the rate of about a million miles an hour, like a huge oval pinwheel. Our own sun and its planets, which includes the earth, are on the edge of this wheel. This is only our own small corner of the universe,

> so why do not these billions of revolving and rotating suns and planets collide? The answer is, the space is so unbelievably vast that if we reduced the suns and the planets in correct mathematical proportion with relation to the distances between them, each sun would be a speck of dust, two, three and four thousand miles away from its nearest neighbour. And, mind you, this is only the Milky Way—our own small corner—our own galaxy. How many galaxies are there? Billions. Billions of galaxies spaced at about one million light-years apart (one light-year is about six trillion miles). Within the range of our biggest telescopes there are at least one hundred million separate galaxies such as our own Milky Way, and that is not all, by any means. The scientists have found that the further you go out into space with the telescopes the thicker the galaxies become, and there are billions of billions as yet uncovered to the scientist's camera and the astrophysicist's calculations.
>
> When you think of all this, it's silly to worry whether the waitress brought you string beans instead of limas.[4]

But this tolerant camaraderie soon turns to anguish when we take our eyes from contemplating the heavens and fix them on the teeming miseries of Earth.

If contemplation of the sheer size of humanity and the endless immensity of the universe can flood a man with the experience of Unbelief, awareness of individual sorrow and tragedy can add a keen twist to the experience. If we sharpen the focus and enter into the lives of individuals, we are confronted, not with the problem of size but with the problem of pain. To open oneself to the universal fact of pain is to experience a sense of outrage and helplessness in the presence of a harsh and impenetrable mystery. And here I can only speak personally again. The experience of Unbelief is not a generalised experience—like Faith, it is a deeply personal awareness. The priest is in a peculiar position to witness what St Paul called the pain and travail of creation. Often, it is a particular experience which captures and typifies the whole. I can remember many such.

I can remember watching by the bed of a young woman with her husband and children as she lay a long night dying. To this day I remember vividly the tender action of her husband as he stroked her forehead and dampened her lips, hour after hour, through that long, last night of her life. I can remember nights and days in other hospitals by other beds. But the occasion I remember most clearly goes back to my first year as a priest. I was invited by a young doctor to make regular visits to a ward in a large hospital in Glasgow. He explained to me that many men in this particular ward had been there for over thirty years. After the First World War an outbreak of Spanish 'flu swept through the world and many people died. This was followed, in some parts, by a disease called *encephalitis lethargica*, or sleepy sickness. Most of the men in the ward I was to visit had contracted the disease in the 'twenties, and had been in hospital ever since. When I went to the ward for the first time I saw why. Some of the men were able to shuffle about after a fashion, but many of them were completely paralysed. Some of them were merely breathing statues, unable to communicate except by moving their eyes. They lay in bed, with a frail spark of life within them, entombed in flesh. By that time their families had either died or lost interest in them, and few of them were ever visited. There was one man there, however, who had been visited by his old mother three times a week for over twenty years. She would come into the ward, put down her shopping-bag by his bed, and hold her son's hand for half an hour, and leave as silently as she came. On that day in that ward I understood for the first time what Paul meant when he said that the whole creation 'groaned and travailed in pain'.

But there is more than the pain of disease. I remember a young girl who was placed in an orphanage. At first she would talk to no one, nor play with the other children. Gradually a friend of mine won her confidence and she blurted out her story. Twelve years old, she was the eldest child of a prostitute. Her mother became pregnant but managed to disguise the fact. At two o'clock one morning she went into labour and the girl had to assist at the birth and deliver the baby. Her mother refused to look at her new-born child. Instead, she sat up in bed and fired off a series of bizarre instructions to her frightened daughter. The baby was wrapped in a thick blanket and placed in an old suitcase. The girl was instructed to take the suitcase and leave it in a deserted building in another part of the city. In a state of shock, the girl did as she was told. But she never returned to her mother. Days later she was picked up by the police, wandering through the city streets, crying soundlessly. The pains of creation!

Think of the millennia of suffering this creation has endured: the millions killed in the wars of this century alone —the flower of a whole generation slaughtered in the mud and carnage of World War One; trainloads of Jews trundling endlessly through the night to fill those graves at Dachau and Belsen and Treblinka. Litanise all the names: Hiroshima and Dresden, Coventry and Clydebank—whole cities on fire; bombs in the night; children mangled in the ruins. And all the wars since 1945, quaintly labelled *local* or *brushfire* by our pin-striped strategists: Korea, Algeria, Biafra, Vietnam, Ulster. Add it all together with all the unknown tragedies; compute it together with the agony of countless sick-beds and all those haunting faces from a million refugee camps. A whole *creation* in pain and travail.

Christians have tended at times to reduce the problem of pain and suffering to the misuse of man's freedom. Even as an answer to the *human* problem this always strikes me as callous or naïve or both, but if it *is* accepted as going some way towards explaining the mystery of human misery, what about the awful pains of the sub-human creation? It was this which particularly appalled the sensitive soul of Evelyn Underhill:

> We can't, I think, attribute all the evil and pain of creation to man's rebellious will. Its far-reaching results, the suffering of innocent nature, the imperfection and corruption that penetrate all life, seem to forbid that. The horrors of inherited insanity, mental agonies, the whole economy of disease, especially animal disease, seem to point beyond man to some fundamental disharmony between creation and God. I sympathise a good deal with the listener who replied to every argument on the love of God by the simple question, 'What about cancer in fish?'[5]

And still we have not done, for we have still to add all our lesser sorrows, all our failures and regrets; all our yesterdays; all the leaves from all the trees that ever were.

> Margaret are your grieving
> Over Goldengrove unleaving?[6]

Much of the time man experiences life as regret and restlessness, and this accounts for the strange power the past has over him. He is never able to contain and relish the present, so he is left with that mysterious faculty of nostalgic recall by which he seeks to understand what he has been. This is part of the fascination the past has for us: old photographs, brown with age, discovered in someone's attic; pictures of people, now dead, caught in a ridiculous moment and no one left to recall it; and newspaper clippings, filled with vivid details of forgotten minor tragedies; old railway timetables, telling of trains that don't run any more; and postcards, old postcards —wet afternoons in Aberdeen in 1920—'having a lovely time. See you next week!'—next week in 1920. Why is it that old things have such pathos? What is the meaning of this strange search through the past? Graham Greene, perhaps more than any other living writer, has caught the mood of piercing regret that afflicts man. The central character of *The Power and the Glory* is a seedy, alcoholic priest, who after months as a fugitive is finally caught by the revolutionary Mexican Government and condemned to be shot. On the evening before his execution he sits in his cell with a flask of brandy to keep his courage up and thinks back over what seems to be the failure of his life:

> Tears poured down his face. He was not at the moment afraid of damnation—even the fear of pain was in the background. He felt only an immense disappointment because he had to go to God empty-handed, with nothing done at all. It seemed to him at that moment that it would have been quite easy to have been a saint. It would only have needed a little self-restraint, and a little courage. He felt like someone who has missed happiness by seconds at an appointed place.[7]

This is certainly part of the fascination of the past—the rarely expressed feeling that back there a clue to the mystery is lying around which we missed. We failed to make a connection at some crucial point that would have made all the difference, so we missed happiness by seconds at an appointed place. The mystery remains undisclosed, though we rummage through our memories searching for the clue.

A related experience is the restlessness that man feels, though it may only be expressed by the romantic image of the fictional drifter, the man without a star. I have encountered this in myself in various ways. Seeing people off on a long journey can produce the effect I'm talking about: a mysterious sense that travelling, somehow, is more significant than returning to the overwhelming ordinariness of life. Hence the strange appeal of railway stations and airports; the piercing nostalgia of a train whistle, high and lonely, somewhere in the night; or the sound of a ship making out to sea. Or it may be that strange difficulty we find in settling down to the ordinary routines of life after a holiday abroad. There is nostalgia for that heightening of consciousness which new places give us, that sense that quite soon we are going to discover that mysterious contentment and belonging which has hitherto eluded us. There's a sense of being just about to grasp it, of being about to stumble on to some mysterious significance. Usually it eludes us. We never discover the appointed place. We are left with an inconsolable longing; inconsolable because we do not know what it is we long for. 'Man that is born of woman hath but a short time to live and is full of misery. He cometh up, and is cut down like a flower; he fleeth as it were a shadow, and never continueth in one stay.' This is the source of our longing and regret, for everything retreats into the past faster than we can grasp it. This is the pathos of man. All that beauty, all those memories, all in the past, fixed for ever with defiant flatness in some old photograph-album. There is nothing firm to which we can cling. We cling for a moment and it is already part of the past. All our loves and regrets shuttle past, 'swifter than a weaver's beam'.

> . . . it came on Chris how strange was the sadness of Scotland's singing, made for the sadness of the land and sky in dark autumn evenings, the crying of men and women of the land who had seen their lives and loves sink away in the years, things wept for beside the sheep-buchts, remembered at night and in twilight. The gladness and kindness had passed, lived and forgotten, it was Scotland of the mist and rain and the crying sea that made the songs . . .[8]

Suffocated by the pain and immensity of life, unable to understand his own existence, to contain it long enough to examine its meaning, man finds himself strangely lost in the wilderness of being. This is the experience of Unbelief. It may never be intellectualised, but it accompanies man as a longing to be reunited with something in the universe from which he now feels cut off, to be on the inside of some door which he has always seen from the outside. It is to experience reality as locked against him. But few men can live with that bleak realisation, so it is small wonder that human culture filters and refracts the desolation in a thousand ways. Men have learnt to huddle together for warmth against the bleakness, they have learnt to dull their senses against the darkness. Who can doubt that man's age-old dependence on drugs is an attempt to dull this strange loss that afflicts him? If you drink enough or smoke enough or inject enough, for a moment you soothe the loss. The tragic irony, of course, is that it takes more and more to achieve the necessary dulling of the pain. The sense of loss increases, and the addict is left with an overwhelming sense of emptiness which nothing can soothe and nothing can fill. He experiences the desolation of reality with an unbearable intensity that can drive him insane. The addict is the frail edge of the culture of Unbelief. He bears in his body the marks of our desolation. He is the sacrificial lamb of our culture.

There are nobler ways of dealing with the experience, of course—art and music among them. Great art and music catch at a man's heart and give him strange glimpses into the secret he spends his life trying to remember; they take a man beyond himself. They seem always to be on the point of opening up for him the mystery which eludes him. But the movement ends and leaves him strangely unsatisfied. The crescendo dies at the moment of revelation, and the heavens never open. Art and music take man a long way, but in the end they fail. They only increase his longing, they never satisfy it.

None of these responses is to be despised or held of no account. They are what men do with their loneliness, and

> Hold them cheap
> May who ne'er hung there. Nor does long our small
> Durance deal with that steep or deep. Here! creep,
> Wretch, under a comfort serves in a whirlwind; all
> Life death does end and each day dies with sleep.[9]

To know all these experiences is to know the chill and shock of Unbelief. They create a cumulative weariness of the heart and mind. The size of the universe, this apparently endless system of systems, defeats man's attempt to locate a private meaning in it all. Man defines himself and finds his significance in a tiny web of relationships to people and places: how can he fit his tiny pattern into the chilling magnitude of space? The sheer, unrelenting vastness of the universe produces in him a state of credibility-shock which simply oppresses him. Who can blame him for simply changing the subject and switching on the television?

But the sensitive man feels more than sheer bafflement as he confronts the universe. He is offended by the apparent absence of pity in the great movement of being. His Unbelief is not fatigue, it is moral outrage, a terrible pity for the small things crushed by a bullying universe. For him, Unbelief is a badge of pain which he wears to defy the pitiless implacability of existence.

There is another major element in the modern culture of Unbelief, but before examining it I want to stop at this stage to find out if Faith has even a tentative word to say to Unbelief about the problems raised so far in this chapter.

3

The Reply

ONE OF the ways in which man's enduring egotism shows itself is in a patronising contempt for the past. This contempt shows itself in many ways, some more amusing than others. Men are always identifying great divides in their history which, they claim, create qualitative differences between generation and generation. The implication always is that back there, beyond the great divide, men were more naïve or credulous in their attitudes to life. Life, it is maintained, presented itself with great simplicity and innocence then. Men were more childlike and ingenuous, more liable to have the wool pulled over their eyes by priest and charlatan. This attitude is very obvious in the history of religious thought. It was always easier for our forefathers to believe in God because they knew less about the universe than we now do. Our greater sophistication and awareness of the way things are create problems which they, poor dears, never had to face.

This discrimination against the past is the only form of discrimination which is intellectually respectable today. The inherent intellectual inferiority of every generation but our own is one of the dominant assumptions of our era. Man has come of age in *our* day, and all who came before were mere children. No matter how fashionable this view may be among men of unimpeachable liberalism, it is really only a form of intellectual fascism. It is yet another manifestation of that radical egotism which is the root of all prejudice and discrimination among men. It is a form of elitism which goes unopposed only because the dead cannot rise in their own defence. Every other form of oppression is challenged today, but this imperialism of the mind is accepted as self-evident. One reason why the modern view has a certain specious acceptability is the phenomenal success men have achieved in the latter part of this century in conquering their natural environment. Here there can be no argument. Men *have* conquered space and most disease and many of the natural hazards of the universe. They have achieved a phenomenal expertise in these things, but they are not noticeably wiser or better or happier as *men*. If man's real task is to study to be wise, then he is no further on in his endeavour. Indeed, certain observers of the modern scene are convinced that man, for all his technological sophistication, is slipping into a new barbarism which places him well *behind* his forefathers in the quality of his humanity.

> Compared with the visionary powers that moved in these souls (the great souls of the past), what is the value of all the minor exactitudes of all the experts on earth? We should reject the small souls who know only how to be correct, and cleave to the great who know how to be wise.'[1]

Another element in the modern view which gives force to its arrogance is the result of a simple confusion. Many of the great visionary myths of history are thought to be the outdated science of the past, primitive attempts to explain the working of the universe. This is a profound and damaging misunderstanding. It is true that many of these visionary accounts of reality did service in a double way, both as interpretations of the hidden meaning of existence *and* as a sort of primitive science, but it was the former which was their real concern. It is true that the guardians of the myth have frequently been too protective of its secondary role, but this has usually been because they were pretty certain that more was at stake than science's account of external reality.

> 'What', it will be Question'd, 'When the Sun rises, do you not see a round disk of fire somewhat like a Guinea?' O no, no, I see an Innumerable company of the Heavenly host crying, 'Holy, Holy is the Lord God Almighty'. *William Blake*

It has usually been the case when the man of vision concedes the unimportant fact to the scientist that, seen with his eyes of flesh, the Sun is 'a round disk of fire somewhat like a Guinea'; the implication has been that it cannot be anything else at the same time, and this the visionary will not concede, though it place him in the clown's role of obscurantist and reactionary. His eyes of fire have seen a depth and wonder in reality which are beyond the range of the contemptuous superficiality of science.

> We must be prepared to entertain the astonishing claim men like Blake lay before us: That here are eyes which see the world not as commonplace sight or scientific scrutiny sees it, but see it transformed, made lustrous beyond measure, and in seeing the world so, see it as it really is. Instead of rushing to downgrade the rhapsodic reports of our enchanted seers, to interpret them at the lowest and most conventional level, we must be prepared to consider the scandalous possibility that

wherever the visionary imagination grows bright, magic, that old antagonist of science, renews itself, transmuting our work-aday reality into something bigger, perhaps more frightening, certainly more adventurous than the lesser rationality of objective consciousness can ever countenance.[2]

This conflict between objective and subjective interpretations of reality will be the main topic of discussion in the next chapter. I have only mentioned it here because many assume that Unbelief has only really been a problem *in our time;* that *only in our time* have men become aware of and been overwhelmed by the magnitude of the universe; that *only in our time* have men had the sensitivity to be revolted by the unceasing agonies of the natural creation. In short, that *only in our time* have men had the wit and the grace to find Faith difficult. This is far from true. Real Faith has never been an easy attitude to maintain; it always involves discipline and the courage to trust even in the face of apparently overwhelming odds: 'Though he slay me, yet will I trust in him'. This is why the Church has said that Faith is a virtue. If Faith were the effortless endowment that many have taken it to be, then there would be little virtue in having it. It is true that the original vision or apprehension of reality as being full of Grace and Meaning comes unbidden as a gift, but Faith is the ability to be obedient to that vision, long after its freshness has failed and the memory of it has darkened.

And this obedience is no easy thing. The original vision is constantly challenged by the pressures of Unbelief and despair. It is true, of course, that there is a purely cultural phenomenon which we might call 'generalised belief', but this is no more significant than its opposite number, 'generalised unbelief'. Faith and Unbelief in their purity are de-

ficantly personal attitudes to reality, deeply felt and leading to commitment to a way of life. They are not simply part of the fashionable mental furniture of an era. In our culture generalised unbelief is the prevailing fashion, just as generalised belief was the fashion in the Middle Ages, but they both bear as much relationship to the authentic reality as does a Boots print to Mount Everest. They are just part of the decoration. Faith *knows* what counts against itself, because it is part of the reality of Faith that it should know it. And Faith has always known it. All the great testaments of Faith, such as the Jewish and Christian scriptures, are full of the data of Unbelief. The Old Testament is full of an overpowering awareness of the immensity of the universe and the frail insignificance of man. 'When I consider the heavens, the work of thy fingers, the moon and the stars which thou hast ordained; What is man, that thou art mindful of him, and the son of man that thou visitest him?' (Ps. 8). And the problem of pain and suffering, too, is part of the very fabric of Faith's own passion, because it rises as an endless challenge to those certainties which are endlessly won yet never entirely possessed. Indeed, as we shall see, the problem of suffering is felt more acutely by the man of Faith than by any other. It *is* Faith's problem. What account, then, can Faith give of itself in the face of these dark challenges?

To begin with, we must enter a major and abiding caveat. Faith cannot and must never attempt to argue away these challenges. They are part of the very data of reality and they cannot be removed by a form of words, no matter how comforting the formula may be. The man of Faith can only say how he lives with these perplexing facts; he can never pretend that he has banished them from the horizon. He cannot. They are a permanent part of the landscape for Faith as well as for Unbelief.

There can be no lengthy or elaborate reply to the problem posed by the size of the universe, or at least none that I can bring. But man's very awareness of its vastness is, in a very real sense, a conquering and transcending of the universe itself. Man's conciousness of the magnitude of reality is a fact of greater significance than the sheer bulk which he contemplates. We can be fairly certain that most of the universe is insensate matter, and that the vast interstellar spaces are just spaces. Man's ability to observe and investigate, to be appalled and humbled by the universe is a more impressive fact than the sheer size of things. He is aware of the universe, but we can be pretty certain that the universe is unaware of him. And the probability that there are sentient beings on other planets does not affect the fundamental point. We do not know what problems they face (though they are very likely to be not unlike our own), but we do know that there are certain values, certain non-material realities, which are of infinitely greater intrinsic worth than all the rock in creation.

The spiritual passion of John the Baptist was an infinitely greater and more mysterious fact than all the sand in the Judean desert. The mind of Copernicus was a greater wonder than the heavens he explored with his telescope. There is great scandal in the fact, but it seems to be part of the very structure of reality that size is not proportionate to significance. C. H. Dodd, in another connection, called it 'the scandal of particularity'. He was commenting on the strange emergence of genius in particular people at a particular time. By some mysterious election, great poets and musicians and religious geniuses emerge out of the general mass of humanity in no easily discernible way. They just appear, and their existence both justifies and enriches the rest of us. The whole significance of mankind, by some mysterious selection process, is located in such men. They are peculiar people, called out to serve and ennoble all men by their particular gifts. Many men have seen a similar process at work in the universe as a whole. This vast system of systems, it is claimed, provides the context for the emergence of a sentient and self-conscious being. He is the end towards which creation has been working. There can be no empirical demonstration of this claim. It is closer to Vision than to Science, but it is a possible response to the riddle of the universe and it is one which confers some direction upon the abundant confusion of creation.

The man of Faith does not claim to know the answer to the riddle of the universe, but he discovers in it all sorts of hints and suggestions which point to an underlying purpose beneath the sheer and apparently senseless plenitude of being. He is aware of experiences in his own life where a tiny gesture has illuminated the whole meaning of his existence, and it is his own existence, after all, which he must make sense of. This personal responsibility for existence cannot await the unfolding of all mysteries, it must be tackled *now*. And it is his own private passion for purpose and direction in life which gives him the strongest hint as to the meaning of all things. Whence does he derive his need for purpose and significance if not from the very reality whose overall purpose he was only now questioning?

Man himself is the strongest argument against his own doubts. He does not wait until the meaning of everything is made plain before doing anything. He operates on the basis of partial and fragmentary insights which give him enough light to go on for the moment. Man lives inductively, that is to say, he discovers from his own partial experience and sense of purpose enough reason for living his own life, without being certain of the overall purpose of all things. If he is theoretically inclined, he may argue effectively from his own experience and the experience of others to a tentative general truth, but the general truth is a result of the private experience. There is no other way to live. It is impossible to live deductively, to wait until the total meaning is declared before embarking upon the adventure of living. That is to try to live life backwards, and it cannot be done. We move, if we move at all, from the meaning of our own life to the meaning of all life. No postponement is possible. We must read the meaning as we run. This is how men live and it is the only way in which they can believe. The meaning of the whole is revealed through the part. Man has no other way of knowing, he has no faculty large enough to absorb the meaning of the universe in its totality, but the totality can be mediated to him through the particular if he will wait upon it. When man humbles himself beneath this necessity, he receives as gift what he could not achieve by his own mental effort.

> To see a World in a Grain of Sand
> And a Heaven in a Wild Flower,
> Hold Infinity in the Palm of your hand
> And Eternity in an hour. *William Blake*

The only answer that Faith can give to the man who is oppressed and puzzled by the size of the universe is the answer given by our Lord to Peter's question about the Apostle John: 'What is that to thee? follow *thou* me.'

If the problem of size is presented most acutely to man's *mind*, the problem of suffering presses most heavily upon his heart, and it is a problem which presses with particular fierceness upon the believer. Dr E. L. Mascall has pointed out the paradox presented by the problem of suffering; the existential question as distinct from the purely academic one occurs, he says, only for the believer.

> 'How', he agonisingly asks himself, 'can a good and omnipotent God allow these things to happen?' For the unbeliever there can only be the academic question, 'What is the basic character of a world in which such things occur?' He may be puzzled and even frightened, but he has no rational ground for resentment; in a godless world there is no reason why anything whatever should not occur, there is no reason why such a world should not be ultimately hideous, and if it is there is no one who can be blamed. Behind the problem itself there lies another problem: if there is no God, why should unbelievers feel there is a problem at all, for many of them certainly do? The point was expressed pungently in one of Ingmar Bergman's films: 'If one can believe in God, there is no problem; if one cannot, there is no solution'. To which we might add: 'If one cannot, why is there a problem?'[3]

Suffering may be a problem for the believer, but it is a problem that arises *as a result of* his Faith and it cannot logically be used as an argument against it. A clumsy analogy from medicine might illustrate this. Let us suppose that I contract a deadly disease which will kill me unless it is checked and controlled by suitable treatment. So the doctors put me on to a drug called 'X' which controls the disease and assures me of a normal life-span. Unfortunately, the drug has certain unpleasant and unavoidable side-effects which the doctors do not yet entirely understand, though they are constantly struggling with the problem. The drug impairs my eyesight and gives me periodic headaches. This life-giving medicine brings with it certain painful and unalterable disadvantages. I can do either of two things: I can continue to take the drug and cope with the problems though I do not like or understand them. Or I can rail wildly against the drug and its manufacturers and their good faith in marketing it in the first place. I can give up the use of the drug. My vision improves and my headaches disappear, and in a few years I am dead.

We live in a mysterious universe. Belief in a good God lights up that mystery and gives it meaning. The fundamental problem of life's meaning is resolved by Faith. But Faith, in turn, gives rise to certain derivative problems, such as the problem of suffering. To give up Faith because of the problems that derive from it is as foolish as giving up a life-giving medicine because of its unpleasant side-effects. In each case the avoidance of the problem only leads to death. The person who gives up belief in God because it brings with it certain unresolvable dilemmas ends up by believing in a dying universe in which there is no meaning anywhere, a universe which came from nothing and goes to nothing, a universe which is cruelly indifferent to all our needs. And there is no point in feeling resentment against such a universe, because in a godless universe there is no reason why anything should not happen, and there is no one to resent, no one to blame.

We are alone in an empty universe. No one is listening to our curses or our tears. We stand, tiny and solitary, in a corner of a vast and empty landscape, and if we listen, all we hear is the bitter echo of our own loneliness. The man of Faith admits that his vision is blurred. He sees the mystery of life through a glass darkly, but he does discern some meaning, and one day, he believes, his eyes will be opened fully and all the painful mysteries of life will be made plain. The man of Unbelief cannot accept this partial and faulty knowledge. He insists on seeing the plans and the maintenance manual for the whole of creation, and when it is not forthcoming he withdraws his co-operation. He rejects Meaning. He breaks the glass. And what is he left with? Thick darkness, the impenetrable blackness of a life lived without hope. He is like a short-sighted man who plucks out his eyes rather than go through life wearing spectacles. At one stroke he crosses out the problem of suffering, but he only succeeds in leaving himself with the problem of life itself.

I said in Chapter 2 that the sensitive unbeliever feels an angry resentment as he contemplates the endless suffering of creation. His Unbelief is a protest against a universe he sternly disapproves of. And this passionate resentment is itself a kind of Faith. On one level it may not be very significant. There is a type of unbeliever who gives up belief because he wishes to punish God for the callous way he handles his creation. Something of this approach is reflected in a passage from Joseph Heller's *Catch 22*. The characters reject belief in God, but they have to bring him back in order to have an adequate object for their moral indignation.

> 'What the hell are you getting so upset about?' he asked her bewilderedly in a tone of contrite amusement. 'I thought you didn't believe in God.' 'I don't', she sobbed, bursting violently into tears. 'But the God I don't believe in is a good God, a just God, a merciful God. He's not the mean and stupid God

you make him out to be.' Yossarian laughed and turned her arms loose.

'Let's have a little more religious freedom between us,' he proposed obligingly. 'You don't believe in the God you want to, and I won't believe in the God I want to. Is that a deal?'[4]

The moral indignation of the Unbeliever usually moves at a deeper level than Yossarian's tolerant cynicism. It can be a real discipline which purges and cleanses the heart and fills it with an enormous pity for the wretched of the earth. Many of the secular saints of this century have been men of this mould, men who have given themselves to the service of their fellows, driven by an anguished love which finds no support from their own convictions about the ultimate structure of reality. Theirs is the heroism of despair. Though they may not themselves realise it, however, their own heroism and indignation provide fascinating clues to the very reality they deny. How can we account for their sense of moral outrage in a universe which is supposed to be massively indifferent to the sufferings of humanity? Whence do they derive the courage to love and serve, if the universe is ultimately hideous and unfeeling? How does pity emerge from this un-echoing emptiness? These problems are as impressive as the problem of evil and suffering, though less spoken of. If we are to allow the problem of evil to state itself with such stark clarity, then we must allow the problem of Good equal time in the debate. And goodness is as much a problem for the Unbeliever as is Evil for the Believer. The data are every bit as impressive. History is filled with examples of heart-wrenching charity and self-sacrifice and nobility. Good men have influenced men and their affairs quite as dramatically as have their villainous counterparts. Even in situations of the keenest misery and deprivation, human love and goodness have shone through with an unconquerable simplicity. Beneath the surface of the great tragedies and convulsions of history, men have loved and served each other with unregarded quietness. And even the sub-human creation reflects this same mystery: the care shown by all creatures for their young; the amazing heroism shown by the tiniest bird in following its strange migrant urge; and the marvellous spectacle of life itself in the ordering of the seasons and the grandeur of the Earth. There is as much to lift the heart in the universe as there is to depress the mind; there is as much majesty as there is misery. Is there more logic in believing the worst possible than in believing the best possible? I am not, at this stage, making a legal judgement between the rival claims, but Faith, on the evidence, need not feel herself to be inadequately protected from the testimony of her accusers. It is not her task to make a case for herself, but when she is challenged to do so she is in just as strong a position as her more pessimistic sister.

I shall return to the theme of suffering in a later chapter, since it is very close to the centre of the Christian Faith, but something else must be said at this stage, however inconclusively. For the Christian believer, a cross stands at the heart of reality. Interpreting the meaning of the cross is an endless task, because it is at the very heart of all things and all value. The law of the cross, the law of triumph through suffering, glory through pain, is a writ that runs right through life. The cross is much more than an isolated event in history on a bleak Galilean Friday. The historical cross was a placarding, a cosmic advertising of the fact that life comes through death, finding through losing. Grains of wheat die in the earth before the green shoots appear. Prizewinning athletes have to die daily in those passionate training sessions, their lungs bursting towards death as they struggle towards the tape. The pianist who dazzles us with such effortless grace has nailed himself to the keyboard for years. That old lady who sits up in bed frail as a bird and glowing with sanctity has endured a life of unbelievable tragedy and privation. In life, each little glory, each small triumph, each stride towards perfection is a way of the cross. It may be impertinent of me to talk of such things. I have endured little suffering in my life, but I have witnessed great suffering in others. And I have seen either of two things happen. Some are crushed by suffering. Tragedy stunts them, makes them bitter and resentful. There are others, and I have known many. I have seen the glory rising in them. I have seen them transfigured by pain, made holy by suffering, cleansed and made fine by endurance. I cannot explain it but I know it to be true. And I think that here we have a hint of the final answer to the problem of suffering.

Just as suffering can be transformed into glory in this life, just as evil can be conquered by the way it is endured, so, Christians believe, one day we shall see the whole agony of creation transfigured into an inextinguishable joy. But that joy and fulfilment will not cancel out the suffering or make it unimportant. Suffering *is* important. It cannot be cancelled out like figures in an accountant's ledger. I remember one bleak winter's day I buried a young child and afterwards tried to find some word to say to his mother. I told her foolishly that there was no way to lessen the pain. She looked at me with fierce tenderness and said, 'I don't want the pain to be soothed. I *want* to feel it. How should I not suffer for the death of my only son?' There is a terrible and essential beauty about suffering. It is part of our condition. It is part of the very mystery of life itself, and how should we not feel it? Suffering *may* pass. To *have suffered* never passes. It is so hard to put this mystery into words, but I believe that at the end of all ends we shall see that not one drop of suffering has been lost; neither the great agonies of war nor the small sorrows of a child will have been wasted. By the mystical working of God's purpose all of it, *all of it*, will be transfigured into that joy which God had prepared for us before the world began. In that day he will say to us: 'You see, my children, it had to be like this, but none of it is wasted, none of it is wasted.'

We *can't* solve the problem of suffering. To solve any problem you need to know all the facts, and we won't know all the facts until the end of time, until God's day. But we do know that in the presence of suffering we are close to the very life of God as he labours without ceasing to prepare a place for us where all tears will be wiped away.

> A woman when she is in travail hath sorrow, because her hour is come: but as soon as she is delivered of the child, she remembereth no more the anguish, for joy that a man is born into the world. And ye now therefore have sorrow: but I will see you again, and your heart shall rejoice, and your joy no man taketh from you. (John 16.21–22).

4

The Myth

CHRISTIAN THEOLOGY has suffered many shocks and reverses in the past century, but the most traumatic shock of all must surely be associated with the name of Rudolph Bultmann and his famous de-mythologising programme. Though Bultmann's method was far-reaching in its effects, it was really disarmingly simple in essence and application. It consisted of a single-minded application of our old friend the empirical verification principle to the historical tradition of Christianity. Bultmann decided that the historical narratives of the Faith had little empirical basis in fact. They reflected the pre-scientific world-view of the first century, which held a simple, three-tier view of the universe, with hell in the basement, this world in the middle, and heaven on the top floor. This wedding-cake account of the nature of reality had obviously had profound effects upon the way the early Church saw and explained the meaning of Jesus Christ. He literally came down from heaven to rescue man from the domination of evil powers who had taken control of this middle-world of creation. This he did by offering himself to the Prince of this World as a hostage or ransom. But the Devil was duped by the bargain he struck, because Jesus was the strong Son of God who could not be held by him. After three days in the tomb, he rose from the dead and ascended back to heaven, having meanwhile descended into hell to liberate those held in torment there.

This account of the work of Christ, Bultmann claimed, made every sense to its first-century listeners. It was couched in a language they understood and it was based upon their own pre-Copernican view of the universe. It was not, for them, picture language. It was their science, their truth. But it is a profound embarrassment to the modern Christian who does not share the pre-scientific world-view of the first Christians. The myth of the three-tier universe has been replaced for twentieth-century man by the objective certainties of science: the universe is a vast and constantly exploding system of systems, in which there is no up or down or middle. How, Bultmann asked, can we liberate Jesus from the confines of the first-century myth so that he can be saviour for men of today? His method was to personalise or existentialise the meaning of Jesus for each man. The Resurrection of Jesus was not a literal elevation from the second floor to the third floor of creation; it was a personal experience of the follower of Jesus who applied the myth to his own private life and pilgrimage. The death of Jesus was the disciple's death to all that was shoddy and secondhand and unauthentic in his existence; and the resurrection of Jesus was the disciple's rising to a new life, in which he courageously lived his own life as his *own* life, with honesty and integrity. The myth of Jesus' dying and rising, by some mysterious chemistry of faith and trust, enabled the disciple to do this. So the dying and rising of Jesus Christ was not something which happened 2000 years ago; it was something which happened wherever and whenever man moved from unauthentic, second-hand existence to authentic living. Of course, the combinations and permutations of the scheme are endless and have been endlessly explored by generations of uncomfortable preachers who clutched at the straw held out to them, with desperate gratitude. Bultmann's thesis was taken up and popularised in the English-speaking world by Bishop Robinson in his famous paperback *Honest to God*.

Now, it is not my intention to offer any critique of Bultmann's programme[1]. It ought to be pointed out, however, that the most devastating criticism of Bultmann is not theological but logical. If the traditional Christian narratives are pre-scientific myth, with no objective or empirical content beyond the probable facts that such a person existed and was crucified, and that attractive echoes of his teaching still reach us through the New Testament documents, what is the *logical* purpose of associating man's duty to live existentially with such slender data? This has never been adequately answered, and the reason is almost certainly that Bultmann either really believed that there was more to Jesus than he appeared to allow (and the *more* would be impossible to verify or validate empirically), or that he retains a nostalgic fondness for the tradition and wishes to maintain as much of it as possible, very much as a sophisticated Roman might have argued for the retention of pagan myths on cultural or political grounds. Be that as it may, I simply want to use Bultmann as an example.

In Chapter 2 I discussed some of the experiential aspects of Unbelief. I now want to look at the most profound intellectual element in the current culture of Unbelief, and that is the sceintific world-view which was the *a priori* basis for Bultmann's demythologising programme. Bultmann is an instructive example. If the prevailing world-view can have such profound effects upon the thinking of a Christian professor of theology, equipped with the intellectual versatility to restate the Christian tradition in a less embarrassing way, what must have been the effect of this way of looking at reality upon those who had neither his versatility nor his personal stake in the question? The effect has been to raise an insurmountable barrier to the very possibility of religious belief in the minds of the most intelligent representatives of our western, scientific culture. The scientific world-view, it is held, posits an intellectual veto at the entrance to any religious view of reality. Central to the scientific culture of our society is the conviction that only that is real which can be empirically verified by our senses. It is this method of investigating reality which has attacked the religious world-view at its very roots. And one does not have to be a scientist or philosopher to wield the method with devastating effect. The raw empiricism of the method has pervaded our whole culture, and delivered into the hands of any drug-store philosopher the ultimate religious deterrent. 'Any village atheist who persists in saying "show me" is in the position to hold up to ransom an entire religious culture, with little expectation that it will be able to fill the price demanded.'[2]

The basis of the scientific method is the conviction that the only way to gain access to reliable knowledge of external reality is by a process of critical enquiry cleansed of all subjective distortion and personal involvement. Science, it is claimed, is based on those 'irreducible and stubborn facts' which remain when all the myths have been filtered through the sieve of empirical validation. Now it must be admitted that many religious world-views have exposed themselves to the withering impact of this method. The long rearguard action which many Christians fought in defence of the literal interpretation of many Old Testament myths is perhaps the best example. I have already hinted, however, that those who defended the literal truth of the myths were perhaps more aware of the real issue in the debate than we give them credit for. What is really at stake in this debate is not the correctness or otherwise of rival claims about the history of the natural world, but the *meaning* and *end* of that history.

Religion has always been vulnerable to critical enquiry, since the Subject of its vision is not available to such a method of investigation. What *is* available is that whole, vulnerable apparatus of analogy and metaphor we call religious language, which seeks to express, though it cannot contain, the mystery which it worships. So the religious man finds himself in the frustrating position of one who exults in the blueness of the river at the bottom of his garden on a bright summer's day, only to be met by a laboratory report prepared by his next-door neighbour who claims to have analysed the substance and found it colourless and uninteresting. The religious man sees the natural world as a mirror and sacrament of a Supernatural Reality, whereas the scientist *qua* scientist sees it as so much matter under his microscope. The frustration arises because both of them seem to be using the same language, and appear to be talking about the same thing, though they are using entirely different modes of awareness. The critical scientist looks *at* creation with a cool and objective eye, whereas the religious man looks *through* creation with a passionate and involved intensity to the mystery beyond. The scientific observer is careful to exclude all but the naked gaze of his mind's eye from his enterprise, carefully suppressing emotion and personality; whereas the religious man gives full play to the non-intellective and intuitive aspects of his personality in his activity of adoration. It is true that we cannot fault the scientist on his epistemology within his own sphere, but we can legitimately ask him if his is the only or even the best way of looking at reality. And we can and must refuse him the right to dictate the terms in which the dialogue between science and faith is conducted. More and more people today are finding the courage to challenge the claim that the scientific method is the only reliable method of discovery. Indeed, the most exciting phenomenon of our era is the growth of a massive movement of protest against the dominance of the purely scientific consciousness.

The most sustained and impressive analysis of this movement or 'counter culture', as it is called, is undoubtedly Theodore Roszak's *The Making of a Counter Culture.*[3] He claims that the scientific method, far from being a uniquely infallible investigative technique, is merely the prevailing myth of our era, and he labels it 'the myth of objective consciousness'. He says that a myth at its deepest level is that collectively created thing which crystallises the great, central values of a culture; it is the inter-communication system of a culture. He maintains that the myth which is accepted without question as truth is the myth which holds real influence over us, and that is why the whole scientific consciousness of our culture is maintained as self-evident by modern man. It is his myth.

> What is essential here is the contention that objective consciousness is emphatically *not* some manner of definitive, transcultural development whose cogency derives from the fact that it is uniquely in touch with the truth. Rather, like a

mythology, it is an arbitrary construct in which a given society in a given historical situation has invested its sense of meaningfulness and value. And so, like any mythology, it can be gotten round and called into question by cultural movements which find meaning and value elsewhere. In the case of the counter culture, then, we have a movement which has turned from objective consciousness as if from a place inhabited by plague—and in the moment of that turning, one can just begin to see an entire episode of our cultural history, the great age of science and technology which began with the Enlightenment, standing revealed in all its quaintly arbitrary, often absurd, and all too painfully unbalanced aspects.[4]

The exciting thing about Roszak's analysis is that, in it, scientific or objective consciousness is, by a process of passionate inversion, subjected to a ruinous comparison with those very methods of awareness which have been the laughing-stock of the hard-headed scientist for generations. Roszak conducts his enquiry into the myth of objective consciousness under three rather daunting headings: (1) the alienative dichotomy; (2) the invidious hierarchy; (3) the mechanistic imperative.

1. According to Roszak, objective consciousness begins its operation by dividing reality into two spheres which he labels 'In-Here' and 'Out-There'. In-Here is that place within the self to which one withdraws if one wishes to have a safe observation-post from which to view reality without being contaminated by it. In-Here is a kind of psychic concrete bunker which the self creates and from which it safely gazes upon Out-There through carefully protected slits. Within this carefully sterilised area reality can be examined without risk of infection and involvement. All dangerous subjectivity is purged from the sterilised area, all those 'murky passions hostilities, joys, fears, lusts which

define my person', are systematically mopped up. When this is done, or when you have persuaded yourself that it can be done, you are honouring the myth of objective consciousness. This emptying-out process leaves as little as possible In-Here and as much as possible Out-There. This is the alienative dichotomy Roszak talks about. The self is reduced to as dense an area as possible from which to observe the sprawling reality of Out-There. The ideal state is when the self is contracted into a 'small, hard ball', impervious to the lure of external reality except as it provides so much empirical data for his clinical investigations. Purged of all passion, he becomes pure and piercing intellect. This alienation permits him to dissect a living animal without tremor or remorse, or to investigate the consequences of World War III with painstaking and sterile efficiency. In a horrifying appendix to his book, Roszak gives many examples of scientific objectivity at work. I quote from a study of the probable results of thermonuclear bombardment on civilian populations, undertaken by a commission in the USA.

> We have deliberately avoided arousing emotions. In this area, which so strongly evokes horror, fear, or hope, a scientist is seriously tempted to relax his standards of objectivity and to give vent to his own subjective feelings . . . While we are deeply concerned with the moral and humanitarian implications of bomb destruction, we excluded them from this book, not because we judged them to be of secondary importance, but because they are better dealt with separately and in a different context.[5]

Roszak notes that 'the different context' has not to date been explored by the author, and we can be quite certain that it will remain unexplored since it is dangerous territory for objective consciousness. The scientific observer must preserve himself from the muddy horrors of fear or hope, since they will invade and complicate the chilling sterility of his investigations. He must fight back the temptation to personal involvement. And when all this is done, when the identity has been contracted into the small, hard ball of the investigating intellect, what is left? Who is In-Here?

> Who are 'you' when you are being purely objective? How did you manage to bring this purely objective 'you' into existence —and how can you be so sure you really pulled it off? Moreover, does this purely objective 'you' prove to be an enjoyable identity? Or is that beside the point?[6]

2. Since In-Here must maintain its safe distance from Out-There, an invidious hierarchy is created which reduces that which is observed to a lower status than the observing intellect. In-Here is the centre of reliable knowledge, while Out-There is a stupid and disorganised mass of data which must be analysed, tabulated, interpreted, verified, controlled, manipulated and ultimately fed into some vast computer which guards us while we sleep. The extreme case is, of course, the Nazi physician experimenting upon his human victims with detached and clinical superiority. But this can no longer be written off as an extreme or abnormal case, because the ethos of objectivity has already gone well beyond areas of limited research. Legions of scientists and military men have dedicated themselves to lives of total objectivity. 'They systematically detach themselves from any concern for those lives their inventions and weapons may someday do to death. They do their job as they are ordered to do it—objectively'.[7]

This invidious hierarchy of observer and observed reverses the age-old relationship of man to nature and rapidly leads to the unbridled assertion of man over the natural creation. Creation emerges as a vast, undiscovered and undeveloped reality which must be exploited and managed by the objective consciousness. The consequences of this alienation and overweening pride are hideous and spectacular. Man has smudged and stained and terrorised the natural creation in the name of a jack-booted objectivity.

> An objective, meaning an alienated, attitude toward the natural environment comes easily these days to a population largely born and raised in the almost totally man-made world of the metropolis. It would be difficult for anyone so raised, including a scientist, *not* to be objective toward a 'nature' which he has only known in the form of tidy, if boring, artificialities arranged by the parks and gardens authorities. The flora, fauna, landscape, and increasingly the climate of the earth lie practically helpless at the feet of technological man, tragically vulnerable to his arrogance. Without question, we have triumphed over them . . . at least until the massive ecological consequences catch up with us.[8]

3. However, it is not only external nature which creates problems for the objective consciousness. Problems appear within the person. The citadel of Objectivity is a precarious place, constantly invaded by the disorganised passions of the Subject. So the objective consciousness sets about creating a really foolproof objectivity, an electronic nervous system that will not be subject to the irritating vagaries of the self: the Machine! It comes to be recognised that only a completely *artificial* intelligence can achieve that secure sterility in which alone perfect objectivity can reside. So, by a subtle inversion, the Machine becomes the standard by which all things are to

be judged. It is the supreme embodiment of the scientific consciousness. 'So we come to the ultimate irony: the machine which is a creature of the human being becomes—most fully in the form of the computerised process—its maker's ideal'.[9]

Roszak ends his gloomy analysis of objective consciousness with the frightening prediction that we may not have to wait for the machine to take over, since humans are already modelling themselves upon their own creation.

> We may only have to wait until our fellow humans have converted themselves into purely impersonal automatons capable of total objectivity in all their tasks. At that point, when the mechanistic imperative has been successfully internalised as the prevailing life-style of our society, we shall find ourselves moving through a world of perfected bureaucrats, managers, operations analysts, and social engineers who will be indistinguishable from the cybernated systems they assist. Already we find these images of internally deadened human beings appearing in our contemporary novels and films. Dispassionate lovers, dispassionate killers fill the movies of Godard, Truffaut, Antonioni, Fellini with their blank gaze and automatised reactions. Here we have the world of completely objectified human relations: people hopelessly locked off from one another, maneuvering their isolated In-Heres around and about each other, communicating only by their externalised behaviour. Each In-Here confronts the other's Out-There with indifference, callousness, exploitive intention. Everyone has become a specimen under the other's microscope; no one can any longer be sure that anyone else is not perhaps a robot.[10]

The steadily increasing horrors visited upon us by the objective, scientific consciousness are a result of a too narrow understanding of human knowledge. Knowledge has come to mean little else than a set of verifiable propositions, but this way of knowing is really only the imperialism of the intellect; it is the domination and subjugation of reality by the mind. Nothing yields its most important secrets to such arrogance, so it is not surprising that modern, secular, self-confident man finds no meaning in life beyond the use he makes of it. The knowledge which makes a man wise or good is not that which is verifiable by the intellect, since that is simply to make man himself the central criterion of reference; there is thus something hideously narcissistic about objective consciousness. The other, more enriching mode of knowing or awareness is sometimes called Revelation, and, to receive it, man must adopt a humble and receptive attitude towards reality. He must open himself to receive its gifts. Unlike the knowledge derived by objective consciousness, this way of knowing is of no *use* to man; it does not and cannot involve the manipulation of reality for its own ends, since it perceives reality as the Other, and the only appropriate response to such a revelation is communion and adoration. It is precisely like that experience of revelation we call falling in love. The lover experiences the beloved as adorable, as having an intrinsic significance which is at once humbling and thrilling. Deep calls unto deep, and there is no dominance or exploitation of the one by the other, no manipulation for private ends. Instead, there is total mutuality, as each discloses his or her secrets to the other. Unlike the superficial knowledge wrested by the objective consciousness, this knowledge is not earned or struggled for; it is revealed, it comes as gift. But it only comes to those who risk themselves by opening and abandoning themselves to the other. Unlike the spirit of scientific enquiry, which ruthlessly preserves the clinical detachment of the self as it preys upon external reality, giving nothing and receiving all, this other way of knowing is a way of self-sacrifice: the subject must abandon himself to the Other, open himself with expectant humility to receive its secrets. And the knowledge thus received is vastly more exciting and enriching than that vouchsafed to objective consciousness, since it is the glorious *subjectivity* of the Other which is revealed, and not merely the details of its surface history. In short, this way of knowing is a way of *love*. Its paradigm is the mysterious relationship between the sexes, the mysticism of love and abandonment.

It is tragic that the imperialistic arrogance of the objective consciousness has persuaded our whole culture that only *its* way of knowing is valid, and in so doing has impoverished almost all of man's sensibilities. It has taught us to be better agro-industrialists, exploiting and artificialising nature to our own ends. As a result our farmers are wealthier, but they are certainly not wiser in the ways of the creation they once partnered and loved. Increasingly they turn our countrysides into vast food-producing factories, silent and dead, except for the neurotic bickering of imprisoned chickens. Man presides over a weird, sub-lunar landscape, sterilised and rationalised by his own triumphant intellect. Creation has closed her secrets against him. The birds have all fled. The magic has gone. Nature has been de-divinised. All we behold, from our air-conditioned concrete bunkers, is an unyielding flatness.

Even in the mysterious area of sexual relations the same writ runs. In no previous generation has so much been known about sexual *technique*. We know how to measure and evaluate and even how to prolong our orgasms now. Modern physiologists, after all, have persuaded men and women, in the interest of objective consciousness, to undertake coitus while wired to a powerhouse of electronic apparatus so that they can achieve a statistical measure of sexual normalcy.[10] We know how to manipulate and stimulate our bodies with the same clinical objectivity we bring to everything else. And in so doing we have created an emotional desert, a vast consumer society of throwaway marriages and loveless encounters, in which we use and discard and demean each other, never really penetrating to the mystery of the other. We are as alienated from each other as we are from the natural creation.

And of course the rule of objective consciousness has eroded and undermined the religious sense. No longer is this done by crusading Unbelief. The myth has infiltrated the citadel of theology, so the erosion is from within. Increasingly, theologians take their orders from the control-centre of modern objectivity. The result has been a whole rash of secular and religionless and godless theologies, in which the sweeping claims of scientific objectivity are accepted as self-evident. The results are as dismal and sterile as a modern computer bank. No longer is man allowed to open himself to the mysterious invasions of the Other. No longer is he to be surprised and overpowered by miracle and ecstasy. He must remain firmly in control of the data, gazing out through his little slits, carefully protected against the unreasonable madness of a reality which is irritatingly indifferent to his minor certainties. Religion, like everything else, must be man-centred, since only he is able to know the way things are. So modern, reductionist theologies are yet another example of the arrogant imperialism of the intellective element in man, and they display the same, clean, functional and soulless characteristics as any other piece of machinery.

The good news of our era is that, more and more, people are revolting against this tyranny of the clinical intellect. They wish, once again, to experience the thrill and ecstasy of participation with creation in the great adventure of being. More and more are returning to real partnership with nature. More and more are exploring levels of consciousness and awareness that are the polar opposites of objectivity. They are ransacking the spiritual traditions of East and West in order to attain to that knowledge which is vision, in order to see with eyes of fire that will burn through appearance to the mystery and terror beyond. They are searching for Faith.

5

The Crux

NOW LET me attempt to state in defiantly unverifiable language what I believe is the crux or central issue in the whole debate which has been the subject of this book so far. The central fact in any religious faith is the conviction that there is a Reality which transcends and supports the physical reality of everything which is available to the examination of our senses. This Transcendent Reality, moreover, is held to mediate itself through the reality which *is* available to our senses. We cannot know Reality as it is in itself, pure and intrinsic and underived. We can only know it, as we are at present, at a second remove, as it were. But though this knowledge or awareness of Reality is a mediated knowledge, it is genuine communion which we receive. We really do *know* and *have fellowship with* that which is mediated. We are not, when we experience this mediation, engaged in something which only affects our imagination, or ability to 'Image' something of which we have never had personal knowledge. The obvious example of *this* type of mediation is descriptive writing. When I read, as I just have, a traveller's description of the city of Calcutta it does not afford *me* a personal experience of that vast and turbulent city. What I am offered is another man's experience and, by the use of my imagination, aided by his vivid descriptive power, I am able to enter into something of the meaning of Calcutta, though I have never been there.

This is not the model I am suggesting for our understanding of the way in which Reality is mediated to man. The technical theological term for the mode of awareness I am attempting to elucidate is 'sacramental'. A sacrament, in classical Christian usage, is a sign which effectively conveys what it signifies. By some mysterious chemistry of co-inherence, the sacrament partakes of the nature of that which it mediates. There is in the sacrament a real, as opposed to a purely symbolic, presence of that which is signified. While the sacrament retains its own outward characteristics, those 'accidents' which are available to the senses, it genuinely conveys at the same time something of that for which it stands. Sacraments are not simply signs which stand for something which is not present. They are not ciphers or counters. They are mediating symbols which effectively convey that which stands behind them. The best analogy is taken from the experience of sexual love. When lovers caress and make love the physical activity is a symbolic enactment *of* their love, but it is also that love itself which is bodied forth. Love is *made*, as we say, it becomes flesh, it is transposed into a physical mode. So the activity of *making* love genuinely mediates through our bodies that which exists apart from the way we physically express it. And there is no other way in which it can be done. In John Macquarrie's phrase, man is 'an embodied existent', and reality can only be mediated to him through his senses. It must be bodied forth, made available to him in the only way in which he can receive it. There is no other way in which he can know.

This is true of our relationships with our fellows. Even so-called extra-sensory perception must abide by this law, though it may short-circuit the process a little by flashing the awareness to that part of our senses we call mind. This law of sacramental communication is the mode by which Reality is mediated to us. We experience creation as a sacrament, as mediating to us that Reality which both transcends and supports it. This, of course, presents us with a major and abiding problem. We cannot get at Reality as it is in itself in order to verify or prove its existence and then, armed with this certainty, evaluate the purely mediated knowledge we receive through our senses. Religious awareness always begs the main question at issue, and this is what frustrates the man who is addicted to objective consciousness. But let me develop the 'offence' even further than this.

Most religious faiths have found it necessary to *name* the overwhelming Reality of which they have become aware: they call it God. Like any name, the name of God is a way of defining or particularising the reality which is experienced. One of the great temptations of religious consciousness has always been to merge or generalise the Reality they perceive in a vague and indeterminate way. So the Reality becomes nothing in itself, but merely a way of expressing the mystery of everything that is. It becomes everything in general and nothing in particular. But this seems to defy and contradict man's unquenchable instinct for entering into communion and relationship with the Reality which is mediated to him. He must needs name it if he is to worship it. By naming it he gives it an intrinsic particularity, however mysterious and limitless he feels it to be in itself. The name God, by defining the particularity of this Reality which overwhelms him, renders the Transcendent accessible. But the naming of God is a fateful step. God, as he is in himself, must have an existence apart from the creation. He *is*, as it were, in his own right. So what is mediated to us of God in his creation is not God without remainder; it is not God in the supreme totality of his being, for that were to make the creation God. So there arises in man's mind an ambiguous attitude towards that which mediates his Reality. The sacramental mode becomes a temptation, for what if man mistakenly *locates* God *only* in his signs? In so-called primitive religions this anxiety does not seem to be present. The naïve worshipper is not concerned about or aware of the ambiguity of the sacramental means of awareness. He celebrates the presence of God in creation with an unselfconscious simplicity which does not question the importance of the gift he has received. We can be fairly certain, contrary to the patronising contempt of modern consciousness, that he rarely confuses the giver with the gift. But once the anxiety has been lodged in the mind, how do we deal with it?

There has been one way of dealing with the anxiety which has been of crucial importance in both the history of religion and the history of culture: it is what might be called the *prophetic* or *protestant* perspective. There is a certain kind of mind which stresses the dangerous aspect of any dual activity. It fastens upon the potential and actual abuses inherent in any situation and allows them a more important interpretative role than the more positive aspects. Knowing what is in man, knowing his bias towards self-interest and radical egotism, it fastens upon the evil uses he makes of any good thing as being a more significant fact than the innocent enjoyment of that which is given. It sees creation as a mine-field through which man must pick his way with anxious care, never pausing to gaze about him and enjoy himself lest he stumble upon some explosive evil. Whole cultures have been built upon this perspective, and it is one of the major historical ingredients in our exploitive technological culture in the West. The protestant perspective has had enormous and far-reaching effects upon the whole of Western man's religious consciousness.

True to its basic anxiety about creation, the protestant perspective fastened upon the truth that God was God *apart* from his creation, and that he was not located without remainder *in* his creation; and it chose to emphasise and dwell upon this truth rather than upon its correlative, namely, that there was, nevertheless, a genuine mediation of God *through* his creation. It chose to dwell upon God's transcendence and otherness, rather than upon his immanence or accessibility. It took upon itself the task of defending the independence or autonomy of God as over against his contingent creation. It chose to dwell upon the gulf between God and his creation, rather than upon God's gracious initiative in making himself available through his creation. There were two fundamental fallacies in this programme, of course. The first was that the champions of God's utter otherness could have had no inkling of that otherness in the first place if it had not been mediated to them in the sacramental mode which they now repudiated. The second was an explicit demeaning of the creation, a condemnation of it as a dangerous rival to the sovereignty of God, forgetting that it was *his* creation and the object of his everlasting love. So there follows a sundering of the creation from God with two fateful results.

The first is a veto upon any natural revelation of God through his creation. The creation becomes opaque to God; it is no longer a vehicle of his real if sacramental presence. Instead, it becomes a danger zone which tempts man away from the task of pure and underived awareness of God. The second consequence follows from this: since man is no longer to enjoy communion with God through the natural creation; since it is no longer tremblingly alive with sudden accesses of his presence; since, instead, it is now a temptation to his heart, it behoves him to conquer and enslave it and render it submissive to his will. No longer a partner with the creation, he now becomes an arrogant and fearful master, stalking the earth and bringing it into subjection, smearing it and blearing it with the anxious compulsions of unceasing toil. He no longer enjoys the creation as a man enjoys a friend. He distances himself from it, the better to exploit and tame it. The consequences of this perspective are very terrible and they are all around us. Man is a conqueror in a sullen and abject creation which bears the mark of his ferocity.

But there is yet more. Having invalidated and repudiated the creation as a genuine vehicle of the divine revelation, man has to devise a way of going round the outside, as it were. He has now placed a dense screen between himself and the distant otherness of God, and a new mode of communication has to be devised. The natural creation comes to be thought of as an endless tennis-net, standing between God and man, and messages have to be lobbed over the net if communication is to be possible. Communion with God becomes an extremely taxing and energetic process, involving endless activity and alertness, constantly frustrated by the smothering intrusions of that hostile barrier. Perhaps the most wearying aspect of the whole business is that each generation has to start the process all over again. There is no way in which man can let up, as it were, and simply enjoy the presence of certain abiding realities. He has to be up and at the net if he is to be really certain that he is receiving genuine signals from that distant and chilling transcendence. Very soon the suspicion arises that all who came before were hopelessly amateurish at this taxing sport. New shots are devised, new angles tried, and periodically the whole strategy of the game is radically revised and the rules are rewritten. The expertise and professionalism shown by the practitioners of the sport are frequently dazzling and, as in any game, techniques improve with every generation. Soon, only the most dedicated and well-endowed are able to maintain the pace of the game, and general interest dies out. This is hardly surprising, when the fumbling amateur is constantly told that he has missed the whole point of the game or that he is still following a hopelessly outdated strategy.

This is what happens to religion when it is completely intellectualised, and this intellectualisation is the final result of the pursuit of the protestant perspective. The only faculty which the protestant perspective finds it safe to indulge is the intellective faculty. The intellect is that part of man which seems to differentiate him most radically from the natural creation. It is the faculty or sense which is at the greatest remove from all the entrapments of the natural environment; so, naturally, it is chosen as being the most reliable ambassador for negotiating with the Almighty. God's mediation of himself to man, therefore, comes to be conceived of in entirely rational terms. It is always a mediation through the mind. The paradigm of this mediation, of course, is the

Word addressed to man's reason. Religion becomes a cool and rational activity; it becomes cerebration rather than celebration.

The irony of the situation is that man's reason is no less flawed and distorted than his other faculties. And this fact soon asserts itself. A religion of the mind soon becomes a censorious religion, strongly given, as the term implies, to the evaluation of the other man's truth. It becomes a religion of narrow vision, harsh in its condemnation of the beggarly primitivism of more ecstatic and less cerebral religions. The openings to Transcendence are constantly narrowed by such a consciousness. God is gradually banished from his creation, and communications from him are only vouchsafed through a rigorous intellectual programme. The creation is desacralised, and all those sudden flarings of the supernatural into the midst of the natural are severely prohibited. The correct theological term for this version of religion is *Deism*. The God of Deism is not the warm and involved Father of all those untidy religions of nature, but the remote and chilly proprietor of a clockwork universe, who has left us all to get on with it while he resides in the icy boredom of unapproachable eternity.

It is no accident that the development of this type of religious consciousness kept pace with the growth of the scientific consciousness and was, in fact, one aspect of the growth of that consciousness. The coronation of the intellect of man and his subsequent disaffiliation from the natural creation is the most significant fact in the history of culture since the Enlightenment and Descartes's fatal resolution that henceforth reason would be the sovereign and only judge of reality. The consequences of this one-dimensional commitment to objective consciousness have already been explored in the last chapter. It must be obvious to even the most cursursory examiner of these trends that they reduce the possibility of religious awareness to vanishing-point. If you banish God from his creation and reduce it to inert matter, patient under man's arrogant exploitation; and if you withdraw man's involvement from the creation back into the concrete bunker of the investigative intellect, then you have placed a double barrier against the sudden inrush of revelation. In the first place, you have taught man that the natural creation is simply so much unyielding matter. You do not expend sympathy upon it or seek to reverence it; you simply push it around. After all, the lab analysis proves it, doesn't it? it is simply a load of old rock and muck. You can't demonstrate the transcendent dimensions of a sacrament under lab conditions, whether it is the Real Presence in the bread and wine of the Eucharist, or the brooding Spirit of God in a garden on a warm spring morning. And anyway, one of the most influential religious traditions has fortified this tough-mindedness by expressly forbidding its possibility. The confluence of these two streams of consciousness has created a culture which is almost impervious to religious vision, because it has locked itself into an underground prison and thrown away the key.

Modern scientific consciousness arms itself against religious vision with an insane yet invincible logic. It is like a man who has taught himself to believe that nothing exists by keeping his eyes permanently closed, and who challenges you to convince him of the existence of external reality before he will open them again. The fact that proof is impossible under the conditions he has laid down simply fortifies him in his dismal certainty. This is the religious man's dilemma. The *proof* of religious vision always comes after the eyes are opened, never as a condition for opening them. The Spirit neither coerces nor will be coerced. Like the cave-dwellers in Plato's parable, men can only see the light when they turn and walk, however slowly and painfully, towards it. Understanding *follows* the risk of faith; it is never given before it. Man can have no understanding of Reality until he opens his eyes and beholds it for himself.

There is a sense in which man has to deny the intellective element as a prelude to Faith. He must humble himself before Reality if he is to receive it as grace. He must turn off the investigative, analytic, inquisitive faculty, and hold himself in wordless waiting, if he would perceive Reality. And this stripping bare of the power and arrogance of the mind is difficult for a culture convinced of its own omniscience and omnipotence. The mysteries of Reality are never wrested by the arrogance of the mighty; they are given to the humble and meek, while the rich are sent empty away. In a profound way, much of the present culture of unbelief is a manifestation of that radical pride which is at the root of man's tragedy. It follows that much modern unbelief is simply an aspect of a larger moral problem created by the overweening egotism of man; and reason alone is a futile weapon in such a context. Tyrants are rarely argued from their seats; they have to be thrown down. The tyranny of the purely intellective consciousness has to be opposed by other modes of awareness such as Faith and Vision, and they dare not let the intellective consciousness lay down the conditions on which the conflict is to be fought.

This is one reason why certain of the more extreme

exponents of the counter-culture choose *ridicule* as the most potent weapon in their attack upon the claims of objective consciousness. There is, of course, a great deal of primitive irrationality in certain of the manifestations of the counter-culture, and certain types of religion have been prone to the same silliness. So it must be clearly understood that I am not trying to repudiate the intellectual element in religion. The intellectual element in religion is profoundly important (as anyone foolhardy enough to hazard a book on the subject is bound to concede), but it is an *element* and a secondary element at that. That is to say, it follows after the original experience as an attempt to order and explicate that which has been given. The derivative and secondary role of the intellect is not only a religious phenomenon; it is a fact that is true of any experience of reality. Reality is there before our apprehension of it and *it makes itself available* to our senses, *all* our senses. One of the most extraordinary examples of the radical arrogance of the purely intellective consciousness is the way in which it persuades man that it is *his* mind which brings reality into existence. Roszak has pointed out some of the aspects of this arrogance in his remarks upon the use of the verb *discover*.

> The scientist's nature becomes 'beautiful' when it has been tidied up and pigeonholed. The achievement lies in the scientist's 'discovery' of this order; the credit belongs to the observing mind. It is a situation which reminds one of the quaint use of the term 'discovery' in relationship to the European voyages of discovery. The phrase suggests that the Americas, Africa, and Asia, with all their indigenous peoples, had been waiting eagerly to be found by the white man. We now recognise the comic ethnocentrism of that view; the cerebral anthropocentrism of scientific discovery is less obvious. But Abraham Maslow offers us one lovely example of the subliminal presumption. He mentions the scientist who

praised a book on 'the difficult subject of woman's sexuality' because it at last took up a subject 'about which so little is known'! He goes on to comment on the psychology of the scientist's nomothetic project: 'Organising experience into meaningful patterns implies that experience itself has no meaningfulness, that the organiser creates or imposes or donates the meaning . . . that it is a gift from the knower to the known. In other words 'meaningfulness' of this kind is of the realm of classification and abstraction rather than of experience . . . . Frequently I sense also the implication that it is 'human-created', i.e., that much of it would vanish if human beings disappeared'.[1]

William Blake said that 'a fool sees not the same tree that a wise man sees'. He was talking of the man of 'single vision' who distances himself from reality, acts the part of observer or onlooker. He was talking, with all the predictive insight of prophecy, of the modern scientific consciousness, with its detached and objective attitude to reality. Is it surprising that such consciousness finds Reality locked against its clinical and irreverent arrogance? Our own experience of relationship with our fellows shows us the truth of this. Real knowledge of another person is never vouchsafed to the clinical detachment of the investigating intellect. On the contrary, this approach locks the other person off within the mystery of his own integrity. He will not yield his secrets to such an approach.

We know a thing only by uniting with it; by assimilating it; by an inter-penetration of it and ourselves. It gives itself to us, just in so far as we give ourselves to it . . . Wisdom is the fruit of communion; ignorance the inevitable portion of those who 'keep themselves to themselves' and stand apart, judging, analysing the things which they have never truly known. Because he has surrendered himself to it, 'united' with it, the patriot knows his country, the artist knows the subject of his

> art, the lover his beloved, the saint his God, in a manner which is inconceivable as well as unattainable by the looker-on. Real knowledge, since it always implies an intuitive sympathy more or less intense, is far more accurately suggested by the symbols of touch and taste than by those of hearing and sight. True, analytic thought follows swiftly upon the contact, the apprehension, the union: and we, in our muddle-headed way, have persuaded ourselves that this is the essential part of knowledge.[2]

The central fact of our culture is that man has bound himself fast in misery and iron under the tyranny of the intellective consciousness. It is this consciousness which tells him how to think and what to think about; it tells him what is 'real' and what is merely 'illusion'; it dominates every aspect of his being; it lays down the terms of every debate, the principles of every 'valid' mode of awareness. And it is a tyranny more appalling than all the purely political tyrannies of history, for they, having killed the body, have no more that they can do unto man, but the tyranny of the intellective consciousness is, first and foremost, a tyranny of the spirit which invades and controls man in the very recesses of his being. One dare not negotiate with a power as cynical and pervading as this. When religion seeks to come to terms with this way of consciousness it ends up as a vacuous inanity, drained of all mystery and power, fit only for the bloodless technocrats it sought to impress. A tyranny of this sort must be opposed; it dare not be trafficked with. I began this book with the half-formed intention of discovering a middle factor in the debate between Faith and Unbelief, a principle of co-inherence, which might help to bridge the gap between the two modes of awareness. I have only now come to realise that there must be war between these two modes of consciousness, and a negotiated settlement is impossible, since it is of the nature of the objective consciousness that it demands unconditional surrender.

The only adequate response to the reign of intellective consciousness is revolution and the positing of an alternative consciousness in its place. The most startling fact of our era is that this seems to be happening even now. If various observers and interpreters are to be believed, we are standing before a great historical watershed or transition, a moment of crisis and climax which will leave man's consciousness profoundly altered. At the moment we are in the midst of the transition and a thorough evaluation is impossible, but a profound and far-reaching cultural transition seems to be in progress which renders a great deal of the philosophy and theology of the past decade strangely irrelevant. The whole 'death of God' movement, for instance, though it has a few surviving outriders, stands revealed in all its quaint and old-fashioned absurdity. The symbols of this revolution in consciousness are all around us, and a brief examination of some of them will help us to understand the phenomenon. And the best way to do this is to return to America where it all started.

America is the great laboratory of social change and experiment, and we find in her recent experiences the paradigm which will assist us in understanding the phenomenon under discussion. The counter-culture emerged in America in the sixties as a style of life which ran clean contrary to the American way. We must, however, add an immediate qualification to that statement. America has always been rich in cultural diversity. The American experience contained two formative and explosive elements which still condition her whole cultural consciousness: the ethnic experience, and the frontier experience. Throughout her short history, the USA has been engaged in the painful process of assimilating and unifying a vast range of ethnic cultures. The process is far from complete. Indeed the assimilation of Black culture and consciousness has only really been attempted in this decade, though there is already a great deal of evidence to suggest that it is already well under way. The other formative element in the American consciousness was the experience of the frontier, the sense of constantly pushing ahead into an almost unlimited territorial mystery. These twin experiences have given American history a turbulence and excitement which has created a specific type of American consciousness: it is experimental, innovative, resilient, tough-minded and sentimental at the same time; it tends to be action-oriented rather than reflective; it is more convinced of man's possibilities than of his limitations; its working philosophy is more idealist than realist; in short, and as befits a society whose working principle is the Protestant work-ethic, it possesses all the energy and betrays the absence of tragic vision so characteristic of the truly Pelagian culture. There is a protean quality in American culture which makes Great Britain seem asleep by contrast. The counter-culture, therefore, must be seen as emerging from and having a continuity with this total American experience. American revolutionaries remain profoundly American even when they are repudiating their own nation. Indeed, they are then at their most American, for America is the only society in which self-criticism has reached the permanence and proportions of an art form. Nevertheless, the counter-culture has a significance that raises it above the usual profusion of cultural trends, because it presents a profound challenge to the very presuppositions on which contemporary American technological culture seem to be based. It does not want to climb aboard the American express or even eject some of its passengers; it wants to get off and move, on foot, into the forest away from the rest of the company.

The symbols of the revolution are all around us. America was a short-haired society, so the counter-culture grew its hair long. America was conservative if casual in dress, so the counter-culture got into riotous and outlandish gear. But these were only symbols. Something much deeper was happening. The young man who grew his hair long and wore jeans and beads was symbolising his rejection of the values of the culture he had grown to despise. In a sense he was wearing a religious habit. When the monk or holy man shaves his head and puts on a robe, these are the outward and visible signs of his rejection of the world and its values. Long hair and beads were the outward and visible signs of the counter-culture's rejection of the American way of life.

Why were so many of the most thoughtful young Americans of the sixties so intent on rejecting the values of their culture? The answer must be that in the sixties modern technocratic, man-centred society stood revealed in all its moral and spiritual bankruptcy. America was the great example of the culture of scientific consciousness. All the great American gifts of hard work, ambition, ingenuity and toughness had produced a society of unparalleled wealth. Yet in spite of this massive application of the intellective consciousness America was a troubled and unhappy society. Abroad, she was bogged down in a war which she seemed neither capable of winning nor of extricating herself from.

It is no part of my concern in this book to offer any moral or political evaluation of the Vietnam War. Nevertheless, the conflict is significant for my purpose, for it is an ironic parable of objective consciousness at work. The Vietnam War was plotted and planned and executed with all the clinical expertise of the most impressive technological establishment in the world. It was the supreme example of the intellective consciousness at war. Aptly it became known as 'the Great Muddy'. Some of the most brilliant men in the world mired themselves in a morass of conflict and indecision from which no clear resolution emerged. And at home America was no happier. Her pursuit of wealth, her passion for crossing the frontiers of science and technology had cost her dear. Many of her cities were disfigured by apparently insoluble problems; her waterways were polluted; her eastern and western seaboards were noisy, congested and uncomfortable. But deeper than all this was a chronic spiritual dissatisfaction, a malaise of the soul which was reflected in the erosion of old values and the moral vacuum which replaced them. The middle-aged American was often puzzled and confused. He had created a way of life which his best sons rejected, often cruelly and thoughtlessly. But their revolt, thoughtless and superficial as it often was, was significant: they wanted a simpler way of life; they didn't want to *do*, so much as to *be*. They were not interested in worldly success so much as in spiritual and emotional satisfaction; they were more interested in values than in possession. So they 'dropped out' in their thousands. It is true that the revolt has now been stylised and commercialised and institutionalised, but it has already effected a profound shift in consciousness and it is still at work.

What is significant for the argument of this book is that, on the whole, the counter-culture bypassed the Church. Instead, it ransacked the bazaar of non-Christian religious traditions, from East to West. It not only took over much of the living tradition of oriental religion; in its thirst for expanded consciousness it rediscovered and resurrected much of the old animist tradition of occidental religion, including the fascinating nature religions and shamanism of the American Indians. There was an exultant determination to open up all the doors and windows which had been blacked out and boarded over by the monotonous tyranny of objective-consciousness. There was a positive lust for experiential religions which would actually alter and expand consciousness, and open the subject to the experience of the Other, however understood.

Of course, it was accompanied by a great deal of silliness and exploitation, and gave rise to a new breed of jet-set gurus who sold various brands of instant mysticism to their gullible and adoring followers. It had its tragic aspects too, as in the incidence of malnutrition among the Krishna Kids; and its comic aspects as in the prevalence of a new kind of injury to the achilles tendon called 'yoga-heel', caused by lengthy meditation on the sacred syllable OM while sitting on the heels in the 'adamant posture'! But the most impressive aspect of the almost frenzied determination of the movement was its conviction of the spiritual barrenness of contemporary Western culture. It did not bother to argue with the mandarins of the technocratic establishment; it simply prophesied against them and posited an opposing consciousness and life-style. This aspect of the movement was typified by the amiable Shaman who performed an intricate and arcane liturgy of exorcism outside the Pentagon in Washington, in an attempt to cast out the evil spirits who had taken up residence in that formidable bastion of objective consciousness.

The fact that the movement largely bypassed the Christian Church is significant. Western Christianity was dismissed as simply one aspect of the tyranny of intellective consciousness. The main thrust of Christian theology in the twentieth century had been in the direction of conforming its message to the presuppositions of the culture. There seemed little hope of finding an ally in a tradition which appeared to have retreated before every advance of secular fundamentalism, till it was left peddling a tepid ethicism dressed up in symbolic language. The game is not over, of course, and there is heartening evidence that the Christian Church is refurbishing itself to meet the challenge presented by the moral and spiritual bankruptcy of Western culture. There is a rediscovery of the riches of the spiritual and mystical tradition of Eastern and Western Christianity. There is a new awareness of the centrality, not only of worship, but of the ecstatic and celebratory experience of Faith. Central to all of this and imbedded in the heart of the Christian tradition, is the towering and un-ignorable figure of the Man Jesus. For Christians, he is the principle of co-inherence which unites our temporal reality with that overwhelming Reality which haunts our consciousness, beckoning us to seek after it and find it. He is the sacrament of interchange between this world and that Other which all men are born trying to remember. He is the clue to the mystery that besets us.

PART TWO

6

The Revelation

BEFORE PROCEEDING further with the argument of this book I would like to retrace some of the steps we have taken. I began by talking about the difficulties of religious language. Language, I suggested, was an agreed system of exchange whereby certain symbols had accepted meanings; they were agreeable representations of certain realities. And they could be verified or validated or 'checked out' by placing the symbol against the reality it represented. It was immediately obvious, however, that religious language was in a peculiarly difficult position. How do we verify or validate religious language when, by definition, the primary datum which the language expresses is not available to our senses in a way which makes empirical verification possible? What we might call 'hostile verification' seems to be impossible. It is obviously not possible to wheel in 'God', for instance, as the substantial fact behind that problematic monosyllable. He is just not available in that way. Indeed, any attempt to limit or define God by our language is self-defeating, for God cannot be encapsulated in some convenient symbol. Obviously, conventional methods of verification are ruled out. Whenever a successful religious verification system is developed it is always at the expense of the original intention of religious language. Since 'God' is not subject to hostile verification, theologians frequently find themselves either in opposition or in total capitulation to the culture. They either stand defiantly by their own understanding of religious language, or they capitulate to the culture by giving it meanings which are acceptable and verifiable according to the hostile verification principle. The most obvious method of capitulation and the most popular in recent theology is the reduction of religious language to an elaborate ethical code-game.

Clearly, this is an unsatisfactory position, since it appears to rule out any fruitful dialogue between Faith and Unbelief. I entered a caution at this stage. Language of any sort was a frail and hazardous means of interchange for all but the most banal of realities. Language was an apt symptom and symbol of man's radical egotism. He could use it to confound as well as to clarify. The religious man felt the ambiguity of language with even keener pain, for he was seeking to represent a reality that vastly transcended his ability to express it.

> The earthly artist, because perception brings with it the imperative longing for expression, tries to give us in colour, sound or words a hint of his ecstasy, his glimpse of truth. Only those who have tried, know how small a fraction of his vision he can, under the most favourable circumstances, contrive to represent. The mystic, too, tries very hard to tell an unwilling world his secret. But in his case, the difficulties are enormously increased. First, there is the huge disparity between his unspeakable experience and the language which will most nearly suggest it. Next, there is the great gulf fixed between his mind and the mind of the world. His audience must be bewitched as well as addressed, caught up to something of his state, before they can be made to understand.
>
> Were he a musician, it is probable that the mystic could give his message to other musicians in the terms of that art, far

more accurately than language will allow him to do: *for we must remember that there is no excuse but that of convenience for the pre-eminence amongst modes of expression which we accord to words.** These correspond so well to the physical plane and its adventures, that we forget that they have but the faintest of relations with transcendental things. Even the artist, before he can make use of them, is bound to re-arrange them in accordance with the laws of rhythm: obeying unconsciously the rule by which all arts 'Tend to approach the condition of music'.[1]

It is at this point that liberation can come for the man of Faith. The task of Faith is not, by a persuasive use of words, to convince others of the existence of a reality of which they had hitherto known nothing. By themselves, words can convey nothing of the reality of God. God's reality has to be experienced, and words come along later to express and arrange, as best they can, the meaning of the primordial experience. The man of Faith does not labour under the necessity of persuading men to believe in the reality of something of which they know nothing. His task is to proclaim and describe, however inadequately, his experience of Reality. He is like the lover who must proclaim the uniqueness and wonder of an apparently commonplace person. The lover and the man of Faith see what other men see, but they see it differently.

So the difficulties of Faith are not primarily difficulties of language; they are difficulties of awareness. These difficulties can be interpreted in two main categories. First of all there was the fact of the *experience* of Unbelief. In the face of the apparently meaningless immensity of life man can experience a credibility shock which stuns him into numbness. No

* My italics.

detectable pattern seems to emerge. The riddle of life remains flat and unyielding. And this shock of Unbelief is fortified by exposure to the fact of suffering throughout creation. This can lead to a moral anguish which fills him with a sort of impotent pity as he faces the unfeeling implacability of existence. The sum of these two experiences is a profound and engulfing sense of Unbelief: not a dry and superior indifference, but a profoundly moral experience of outrage against the universe. This is to experience Unbelief as protest. And I suggested that this experience of Unbelief was a profound and unalterable fact of existence. It was one of the ways in which reality mediated itself to man. It was a highly responsible and appropriate response to the reality that confronts man. It was the dark sister of Faith, and as such had to be treated with reverence and respect by the man of Faith.

Nevertheless, there was a possible and cogent reply to this experience, which Faith could make though it had to make it sensitively and with reverence. It was possible to experience and interpret reality in a way which led to the opposite, though related, conclusion of Faith. Patterns and significances and transfiguring experiences were detectable in the midst of the apparently meaningless plenitude of being. Indeed, the very emergence of moral protest within the alleged meaninglessness of life was itself the strongest argument against Unbelief. There was, therefore, a profound paradox at the heart of passionate Unbelief. While no judicial verdict was entered in the debate, I did argue that Faith could give a strong account of itself in this particular encounter.

A much more challenging opposition was presented by the second major obstacle to that awareness we call Faith. This was the result of the imperialism of the intellective faculty in interpreting reality. Citing the work of Theodore Roszak, I argued that the purely intellective consciousness presented an almost invincible opposition to Faith by ruling out the very possibility of any way of knowing other than the detached and analytic, investigative technique of scientific research. This attitude to reality created a profound alienation between man and everything else; and the very method guaranteed the conclusion it sought to demonstrate. Using an analogy from personal relationships, I tried to demonstrate that we only ever come to know another person by humbly and patiently waiting upon him to *reveal* the mystery of his personality by a free response. While the single-minded application of the scientific method might produce a great deal of information *about* the other, it could never plumb the mysterious integrity of the person as he was in himself. The arrogant application of the purely intellective faculty simply reduced everything to a list of ingredients, while leaving the meaning of the whole uninterpreted and inviolate. By the same token, the rule of objective consciousness closed off the meaning of Reality as a whole, and guaranteed its own ignorance by a proud insistence on its own reductionist technique and no other. This type of consciousness, which has permeated and polluted our whole culture, has created a brass wall of indifference against the type of awareness we call Faith. I argued, moreover, that there was little point in arguing with it, since it always insisted on the terms in which the debate must be conducted, *and these terms always guaranteed its own conclusions.*

The exciting and challenging fact of our era, however, was the emergence of a profound movement of protest against this dismal tyranny of the intellective consciousness.

This protest had largely bypassed the institutional churches, partly because of a profound ignorance of the spiritual resources of traditional Christianity, but largely because the churches themselves had appeared to acquiesce under the rule of objective consciousness, by meekly reducing their own basic convictions about reality to vanishing-point. What is required in this situation is an exultant reassertion of the Christian interpretation of reality. Taking a leaf out of the guerilla manual of the counter-culture, this reassertion ought not to take the form of a craven acceptance of the dominant assumptions of the era as terms for negotiating with the principalities and powers of the intellective consciousness. At that game and with those terms we shall always be beaten. No negotiation is possible with a tyranny which is proudly insistent upon its own right to rule. There must, instead, be a revolutionary positing of another, alternative interpretation of reality. There *is* a time for negotiation, but this is not it. This is a time for battle. A whole series of counter-interpretations of the meaning of reality is being offered today, in a time of massive cultural disintegration and transition. This is a day for proclaiming the Christian awareness with defiant clarity. Central to that awareness is the towering and unignorable figure of Jesus Christ. What follows is one man's understanding of that Man as he has received it from the tradition of historic Christianity.

To begin, let me reaffirm a general truth: the whole created universe is charged with the power and grandeur of a transcendent Reality. No form of words can capture the Reality which lies behind that bald and woefully inadequate statement, so let me blunder on even more foolishly. The natural creation, the matter of the universe, is sacramental. A sacrament is a sublime mode of interchange, whereby a spiritual reality is truly conveyed by means of a physical vehicle. I suggested in Chapter 5 that no other method of communication between us and Spiritual Reality could work. We are embodied beings, and any communication with us must respect and operate within the limitations of our nature. We can only receive knowledge of and information about external reality through our senses, all our senses. This is the sacramental principle and it lies behind every method of human communication. We can only penetrate the mystery of other people by perceiving and interpreting the signs or signals they offer to our senses. Human culture is a varied and complex series of sacramental structures. The poet, artist and musician express their awareness of reality in a mode which we can receive. It does not remain locked up in their private vision. It expresses itself, is bodied forth in a medium we can apprehend. Their art is the outward and visible or audible expression of an intense inner experience and awareness. Their mode of communication is, and must be, sacramental. It obeys the laws of embodied or corporeal existence.

But this sacramental method in human culture is but a shadow or reflection of a profounder fact. The universe itself is a sacrament of Transcendence. It is a vast network of signs and symbols of a Transcendent Reality which seeks to communicate itself to men, if they will be seek after it and find it. And the same discipline is involved as in all poetry and art. We must tutor ourselves to read it aright or see it in the correct way. A sacrament never coerces. It is simply there, offered with undemanding humility. To receive it aright, the recipient must stop, linger and interpret the sign and partake with a humble gladness. It will be immediately obvious how vulnerable the sacramental mode is to the arrogance and impatience of man. It calls for a disciplined and searching eagerness from those who would benefit from it. It fills the hungry searcher with good things, but the rich and self-satisfied it sends away empty and scornful. Ours is a rich and self-satisfied culture, too impatient to wait for and interpret these frail signals of Transcendence which are meekly laid beneath our feet. This is what Blake meant when he said that 'a fool sees not the same tree as a wise man sees'. The wise man, the see-er, sees a tree aflame, alive, ringing with the unendurable glory of the divine presence; he sees the tree as a living sacrament of Transcendent Spirit. For such a man the whole universe is a sacrament of God's presence. But the fool sees the tree only as a natural *object*, to be utilised in some way, or summarily felled to make way for motorway or housing estate.

There have been men in every generation and in every religious culture for whom the central and controlling fact of existence has been this Transcendent Reality which meekly and tentatively seeks to communicate itself to man. We call such men mystics or visionaries, and they have enriched the whole human race. They narrow their lives down to a single, overriding passion of longing for the Ultimate which lies behind all the things that do appear. We have, in most cases, the flaming record of their search for and discovery of this overarching Reality which embraces all men.

> If the great Christian mystics could by some miracle be all brought together in the same place, each in his habitual environment, there to live according to his manner, the world would soon perceive that they constitute one of the most amazing and profound variations of which the human race has yet been witness.[2]

Today there is an increasing interest in and hunger for the mystic's experience of the Reality he has given his life to.

But most of us view the spectacle of these single-minded visionaries with a certain wistfulness. Their experience seems so totally at variance with our own meagre longing for the same Reality. Their passion and discipline at once fascinates and appals us, for we are certain we cannot pay the price they gave so gladly for the supreme vision. Is there no middle way between the arrogant indifference of objective consciousness and the self-destructive intensity of the mystic? Is there, perhaps, a low road to God, for those who have no head for heights? And most of us, at some time in our lives, really do long to know God, but we have enormous difficulties in getting to know Him. We feel all sorts of blocks or veils between ourselves and God. We *want* an awareness of his presence, his reality. We'd really like to be absolutely confronted by his undeniable reality. Everything then would be so different. We'd *know*. We'd be *certain*. and everything else would fit into place. We'd then be able to endure anything and overcome everything because we'd be armed with this glad certainty. 'I *know* that my Redeemer liveth', we'd say, and we'd laugh at the sorrows and difficulties of existence. Think about what it would be like to have an unfailing sense of that joyful and unconquerable presence! Though we can but grasp the fringes of the experience, we can see what it could be like when we look at the saints, men and women for whom God is the central reality of their lives—and what an incredible lot they are! One saint, one man alive with the certainty of God's presence, can stand against a whole nation and conquer it—and they have! Such men have changed the face of history: 'Who through faith subdued kingdoms, wrought righteousness, obtained promises, stopped the mouths of lions, quenched the violence of fire, escaped the edge of the sword, out of weakness were made strong, waxed valiant in fight, turned to flight the armies of the aliens.' Oh, to have that invincible awareness! Yet we are all meant to have it. The whole creation is meant to convey it to us. Every blade of grass, every flower, every star conveys, for those who will receive it, the real presence of God. The universe is charged with the grandeur of God; it trembles with the eager certainty of his presence; it is aflame with his love. Those who have eyes to see, see not as we see. They see the same universe, but they see it not as we see it.

But we are not in so desperate a situation of blindness as we sometimes seem to think. Most of us, like St Augustine, have known, at some time or other, Him for whom we have all along been searching. We all have had flashes or intimations of that Reality we secretly or openly long for. Our difficulty is that we have, by and large, lost or severely impaired our ability to *see* Reality consistently, as it really is and not as we have been taught to think it is. This is the most tragic aspect of the radical selfishness which characterises us: we have ceased to be able to see Reality as it really is. Man is so intent on his own purposes of either work or pleasure that he never really sees the creation he inhabits *as it is in itself.* He is like one of those tourists who *do* Europe in ten days: always on the move, travelling, checking in and out—'It's Thursday, so this must be Rome'. And in fact the natural creation which is all around us has a dimension which opens out into the world of Spirit, the world of God. Most of us get occasional flashes of this at odd moments in our lives. When we are in love, for instance, everything becomes charged with a new and luminous and completely indescribable significance. Sometimes a scene of great beauty will evoke the experience; sometimes a piece of music. It can happen at the oddest moments and come unbidden in the most unlikely places. Some time ago I was walking down Shaftesbury Avenue in London, amidst the noise and confusion and apparent absence of all pattern and meaning. I was looking at all the people as they hurried past—all apparently unconnected and estranged, a city of colliding, unconnected strangers. And suddenly I had a flash of awareness: I *saw* the underlying unity between everything there in that congested street; everything seemed to be in place, like some carefully planned and executed ballet; and everything was at one, harmonious. The awareness passed, of course, but it left me elated and with the friendliest of feelings towards everyone. I felt a brotherhood with all that was. George Mackay Brown describes a similar experience, this time in the heart of the austere beauty of Orkney. In one of his best-known short short stories he describes a moment of illumination as it came to Jean Scarth, unmarried, and expecting a child:

> Jean sat alone at the top window of the Ingsevay Inn. Through the window, the hill darkened. The sky was grey.
>
> For four months she had lived in this room. She had neither shown herself outside nor in the bar below. She was dedicated to loneliness.
>
> She sewed in a chair beside the window. She waited.
>
> The days darkened round her.
>
> In her womb the slow shameful inexorable dance went on.
>
> But now the shame had died. She was simply indifferent. Indifference lay on her like a heavy stone.
>
> The hill darkened.
>
> Suddenly she saw the first snowflake. It fluttered over the rose bush in the garden. It climbed the air, circled, meandered

down the wind. Then surely, gently, chastely, it drifted on to the window and clung there, shimmering.

This was beautiful!

Startled, she looked at the frail grey thing on the window-pane. The dead stone lifted inside her.

And then suddenly everything was in its place. The tinkers would move for ever through the hills. Men would plough their fields. Men would bait their lines. Comedy had its place in the dance too—the drinking, the quarrelling, the expulsion, the return in the morning. And forever the world would be full of youth and beauty, birth and death, labour and suffering.

The child moved inside her in a wind of light . . .

The snowflake lived on her window for five seconds, then died into a glistening drop of water.[3]

We treat these experiences as abnormal. Yet how wrong we are, because they show us reality as it *really* is; and what we call our normal awareness is really an abnormality, a terrible short-sightedness, a wasteful shrinking of our capacity for awareness. The creation is a sacrament of God's love; it is a spiritual reality which we can perceive, if we will but learn to look at it aright, and those fugitive moments of illumination we sometimes have are like gaps in the cloud which show us the green land below. The clouds thicken again and we forget the glimpse of that strange and colourful world beneath and assume that this dull grey stuff which is all around us is *reality*! We must learn to look through this reality till we perceive that other dimension of depth. Like the optical illusion, we must gaze and gaze with attentive patience till the flat surface yields its concealed depth.

This *active* way of seeing is painfully difficult and requires a patient and insistent discipline. It is painful because it involves a gradual transfer of interest from the self, the ego, to that other Reality which exists apart from our apprehension of it. And the self operates on the fundamental assumption that *nothing* exists apart from its apprehension of it! Nothing *is* until my observation calls it into being. I don't really believe that other things have a reality or existence in their own right: they just disappear when I am not there to perceive them. It is part of my terrible self-centredness that this should be so. I am only *really* convinced of my own significance, and other people or realities are important only as they relate to *me*, never as they are in themselves. This is man's radical blindness. So the real nature of other people or the natural creation is locked off from him because he never allows them to show themselves to him *as they are in themselves*, because that would involve recognising *their* importance, *their* centrality, and that makes them profound rivals to the self, independent realities. This is why the completely selfish person can never get to know anyone—because he does not really believe they exist in the first place! They are there only for the self's benefit. Many of us, in fact, *live* like this for most of the time, with everyone and everything else as simply walk-on parts or scenery in the great drama of which we are the central character, the hero in an endless television soap-opera. It is obvious, therefore, that this act of looking at reality patiently is a great threat to the self because, to be effective, all the interest must be shifted from the self to what is before us; we must deny our*self* and all its insistent screams for attention and allow the Other to become truly central. To learn to contemplate Reality as it is in itself *and not just as it affects me* is to discover a whole new creation; it is to *see* for the first time.

But even if we train ourselves with painful and unremitting effort to see in this way (and few men have the heroic patience required for this training in awareness) we are still left with an enormous difficulty. The object of our awareness, the reality which blazes slowly behind the signs which confront us, remains vague and uninterpreted. We may have stumbled upon the house in the forest where the fire in the hearth burns brightly and all is laid in ordered serenity, but who is the Householder and what is He like? This is the question we are born asking.

The answer does not come through the general but through the particular. The meaning of the whole is revealed through the part, respecting, as ever, the limitations of our nature. We can vainly traverse the whole world seeking for that which can be revealed to us in a grain of sand. This is the wisdom behind all those mystic traditions of the Quest for the small key that will unlock the meaning of all mystery. They all involve a mode or discipline of concentration, of gathering the self together into a single cone of perception. Whether it is the inward search for that still point or apex of the spirit in man, or the outward search in the old alchemical tradition for the elusive Philosopher's Stone, all share this nameless certainty that the path to the Many and the Manifold is by way of the single entrance and the lowly door. This craving has haunted man's consciousness for centuries. It is what C. S. Lewis called one of man's 'good dreams'. And the dream is fulfilled in Christ. He is the Way and the Lowly Door. He is the certain opening to the Reality which haunts us. In Him the Beyond has come into our midst. He is the crack between the worlds through which we see Eternity.

The best way to understand any reality which is strange to us is to compare and relate it to something which we *have* experienced. Theologians call this the analogical method. It is the only way in which man can talk about heavenly things or, for that matter, about anything at all. We define by likenesses. I want to use this method in trying to interpret the significance and impact of Christ upon those who know him. I have already referred to certain fugitive experiences which most men have had. The most common is that mysterious heightening of awareness we call 'being in love', with its strange power to transfigure commonplace reality. Allied to this experience is the artistic vision of pattern and meaning in the apparently disordered profusion of being. But these types of experience are both essentially unlocatable and almost impossible to command at will. We catch them on the wing, if we catch them at all, and they bear us away to nameless heights, and when we are set down again it is hard for us to say where we have been or how we got there. Are there, then, no experiences of this sort which we *can* return to almost at will? Is there any way in which we can regularly *locate* some brief element of the experience of Transcendence and use it as a frail paradigm of revelation? I think there is, though I may be speaking entirely for myself. I believe that there is a strange *mysticism of place*, and an experience of it can give us at least a tentative analogy for interpreting Christ.

Spiritualists claim that certain places are 'thin'. They mean by that strange expression that certain places are near or on the frontiers between the dimension of this world and what they call the 'spirit world'. Without necessarily accepting their interpretation of the phenomenon, I think we can usefully borrow the term, for certain places are, undeniably, 'thin'. There are particular spots or whole areas where the Transcendent Reality which infuses all things seems to be just below the surface of tangible reality and where it confronts us with a solid and unignorable power. They are places where the boundaries between this reality and that other Reality are thin or non-existent. Men have traditionally called them *holy places*, and not only because they are frequently associated with particular revelatory events. The desert is such a place, and it is no accident that for centuries it has drawn men from all religious traditions as an appropriate place for meeting that Reality they longed for. In the desert the self is diminished and brought low and made aware of the austere mystery of Transcendence. But there are less forbidding examples of the same phenomenon. Certain islands, such as Iona, have the same quality, albeit in a lighter and less terrifying mode. Here the Transcendent Reality communicates itself with an austere challenge that is yet warm and strangely joyful. And there are many places like these. In other days they became places of pilgrimage, tiny parables of that undying conviction of mankind that Reality can be met at a quite tangible location in time and place, that it comes to man in an empirical mode, if he could but find the secret access.

I would take this mysticism of place even further, and suggest that there are certain *buildings* which partake of the same nature (*pace* the Society for the Instant Demolition of Irrelevant Institutions!). I can think of many, but my own church of Old St Paul's in the city of Edinburgh will serve as a simple example. You come in from the unremarkable urban grubbiness of Carrubbers Close or Jeffrey Street, and you cross a mysterious and indefinable frontier. Ordinary folk call it 'atmosphere', but it is nothing contrived; it mainly consists of an unforgettable sense of Presence. It is a fusion of the loving work of men's hands and centuries of prayer, with that Presence which longs to communicate itself to man. It is a meeting-place, a thin frontier between the worlds. And many churches and temples share the same role; they are all in the same place, set upon the same frontier.

This mysticism of place is a remarkable phenomenon and one which can help us to interpret the significance of Christ. All these places have a double nature. They are all clearly in this world, composed of destructible matter, yet they convey a sense of a Reality which is indestructible, eternal. They are stones and sand and brown earth, yet they are something else besides. They are two realities in one; Eternity in time; the Universal in the particular; the All in the one; the Changeless in the transient. And all this is a parable and paradigm of Christ, because in him men felt themselves confronted by the same phenomenon carried to an ultimate degree. There was in him a complete fusion and union of the two realities. He did not just convey a *sense* of that other Transcendent Reality; he *was* that Reality; and at the same time he was of this reality. He was part of the natural creation. He knew hunger and thirst and joy and sadness. He grew weary. He was a man among men. Yet in that man the boundaries between the worlds had vanished. He was experienced as man and at the same time as the full and awful power of God. Men found themselves *worshipping* him, and they were men who followed a religion of the most austere monotheism. In him the power and presence of the everlasting God had broken through in its totality.

It would be easy at this point to lard the argument with numerous quotations from the New Testament, all underlining the central conviction of the Christian tradition that Christ is 'the radiance of the glory of God, flawless expression of the nature of God, himself the upholding principle of all that is'.[4] But to do this would be only to beg the question, not to lend it evidential support. The New Testament, after all, is the account which Faith gives of itself; it is already the testimony of belief. And this is so, no matter what critical perspective you bring to the account. As is well known, Christian scholars bring a bewildering variety of attitudes to the interpretation of the New Testament, and if we wait upon a scholarly consensus to emerge we must wait in vain.

Fortunately we don't have to, for a great deal of the scholarly work which is done on the New Testament, while fascinating and frequently profitable, is religiously beside the point. Apart from those who dismiss the New Testament record as of no historic value and those who accord everything in the record equal historic importance, there are two broad attitudes to the New Testament tradition among Christian scholars. The moderate-conservative attitude takes the record largely at its face value and, allowing for the inevitable confusions and contradictions inherent in any human account of great events, they allow the New Testament writers a high degree of documentary accuracy in their account of Christ. When, for instance, John records that Jesus said to Philip: 'He that hath seen me hath seen the Father', they see no good reason for not accepting the Johannine account of that particular event as a faithful record of what actually happened. The record states it, and the record stands. Their method is consistent and, in its way, highly successful. It begins with a strong positive conviction that the record is reasonably accurate as it stands unless irrefutable evidence to the contrary is clearly led. Their working criterion, then, is a strong presumption of accuracy in New

Testament reportage. It is the prosecution which has to prove the opposite and prove it beyond a reasonable doubt, and, in the nature of the case, this they are not able to do, since it is impossible to subpoena the original authors and interrogate the eyewitnesses of the events in dispute. It would be a mistake, therefore, to dismiss the moderate-conservative attitude to the New Testament as evidence of fear or intellectual dishonesty. One does not have to call the complete roll of the moderate-conservative hall of fame to prove the point. Scholars like E. L. Mascall, A. M. Ramsay and Joachim Jeremias, to name only three, are not notoriously deficient in intellectual or moral stature, yet all, in different degrees, adopt a moderately conservative and accepting attitude to the New Testament records.

At the other end of the spectrum is a more radical attitude to the New Testament. Scholars of this camp bring, in greater or lesser degree, a strongly sceptical predisposition to the historical authenticity of the records. Their working principle is a basic conviction that the records must be presumed unauthentic till they are proved authentic beyond reasonable doubt. This approach has given rise to various tests of authenticity, all of which bear a strong presumption that most or many of the sayings attributed to Jesus arose, in fact, in the early Church and were read back into the record. For instance, Perrin's famous 'criterion of dissimilarity' only allows authenticity to those sayings which cannot be derived either from the early Church or from Judaism. It is rarely suggested that the early writers were 'cooking the books', as it were, only that they unselfconsciously wove together authentic material, with the considered meditations of the first Christians under the inspiration of the Risen Lord, into impressionistic narratives rather than straight reportage. This disavowal may appear to some to be puzzling and disingenuous, however sincerely intended, but it does represent the attitude of much current scholarship.

But who are we to choose between the apparently opposing points of view, if we have neither the time nor the scholarly ability to investigate the dispute for ourselves? I strongly suspect that most of us, including the apparently objective scholars in question, instinctively choose sides in the dispute and muster arguments to support the position we have taken up. Each position is strongly based on certain, strongly held *a priori* assumptions, and, as in much apparently *objective* intellectual research, the succeeding investigation only serves to bolster attitudes largely adopted on other grounds. One thing is certain, there can be no final resolution of the dispute, since all the original witnesses are dead and cannot rise to arbitrate between us and, as C. S. Lewis observed, when we get to the other side we are likely to be too busy with St Peter to interrogate St Mark! We can be certain, therefore, that scholars will go on indefinitely building vast conjectural edifices upon the shifting foundations of an endless series of unprovable and *undisprovable* hypotheses. It is, after all, a fascinating pursuit and there's quite good money in it. The question is, does any of it matter a tuppenny damn? I am strongly inclined to believe that it doesn't, because the main point lies entirely elsewhere. The life-or-death fact will not and need not wait upon scholarly exegesis or eisegesis. It is there before our eyes, and this is it: however we interpret or evaluate the historical evolution of the New Testament record, it sounds one massive note. Variously orchestrated and diversely expressed, it trumpets the fact that in Christ God had fully expressed and revealed himself. To dispute about the exact historical provenance of the Christological claims of the New Testament seems massively beside the point. Whether Christ originally made most of the claims for himself or whether they were simply made about him is a debate we can safely bypass for the moment or for ever. The life-and-death question is, are the claims *true*, and can they be true for me? The unavoidable fact is that *this is how his followers saw him*, and they burned their convictions on to the pages of the New Testament and into the hearts of the first Christians, and the fact has haunted history ever since. They claimed that in Christ that elusive and haunting Reality had opened itself out and that they had actually *seen* and *handled* it! They were not arguing. How *can* you argue a claim like that? They knew how inadequate were the words they used. In the testimony of St Paul you can *feel* the passionate and tortured frustration he endured in trying to set down even an echo of the experience. Even so, they have given us a record of their flaming certainty in words that still exalt and transfigure language itself.

The Christian tradition makes a double though connected claim about Christ. Its main and original claim was about the person and nature of Christ himself. He confronted them with an intrinsic and unavoidable majesty that claimed their worship and the total surrender of their lives. They were forced either to abandon their whole lives to his service or to reject him with a frantic yet wistful haste. He was totally unignorable. He still is.

And because of his unavoidable authority, his teaching opened to them the very heart of that Reality men have spent their history seeking to understand. Here, at last, was reliable news from that other country which haunted their imaginings; reliable, because he imparted an indisputable sense of *knowing* what he talked about. 'Never man spake like this man.'[5] 'He taught them as one having authority'.[6] He was *from* that other Reality and his tidings were reliable. He knew whereof he spoke.

I want to reverse this order of importance in what remains of this book and look first at Christ's teaching about God and, only then and in connection with it, to examine the meaning of his own ministry of service, death and rising again to present and abiding glory. And I cannot state the enormity of the claims I shall be making with greater or more tranquil defiance that the opening words of the First Letter of Saint John:

> We are writing to you about something which has always existed yet which we ourselves actually saw and heard: something which we had opportunity to observe closely and even to hold in our hands, and yet, as we know now, was something of the very Word of life himself! For it was *life* which appeared before us: we saw it, we are eye-witnesses of it, and are now writing to you about it. It was the very life of all ages, the life that has always existed with God the Father, which actually became visible in person to us mortal men. We repeat, we really saw and heard what we are now writing to you about. We want you to be with us in this—in this fellowship with God the Father, and Jesus Christ his Son. We must write and tell you about it, because the more that fellowship extends, the greater the joy it brings to us who are already in it.[7]

7

The Autistic Universe

WHY IS it so difficult to know God? If God is really our great need and if he himself so desperately loves us and made us for himself, why is it so difficult to find him or even to find the right way to him? Why has he put all these obstacles in our way? Why isn't the spiritual life more attractive and the need for God more self-evident? Why is it so easy to avoid God, to disbelieve in him, neglect and ignore him? What is it that stands between us?

These questions raise one of the most mysterious problems that face the follower of any religious faith. The facts are plain, and they are plainly paradoxical. On the one hand there is our need for God, our vague and inchoate longing for him, our inability to achieve peace or fundamental harmony without him. And on the other hand there is the great difficulty we find in realising the true object of our longing and, when we do perhaps realise it, the immense difficulty we find in living our lives consistently according to that realisation. How do we account for this strange paradox? Does a loving father make it difficult for his children to know him and turn to him? Does he play hard-to-get? Well, why does God? Why is there this mysterious gulf between us?

To attempt an answer to these taxing and enduring questions, I want to suggest several analogies or images, all within the canon of knowing God by analogy or likeness. To begin with, the Bible and the universal memory of man are quite certain that there was once complete harmony between God and his creation. The book of Genesis, for example, tells us that God 'saw everything that he had made and, lo, it was very good'. And most religious traditions have this same folk-memory of a golden age. Of course we are dealing here with myth. A myth is a symbolic way of conveying truth, and we are dealing here with a reality that cannot be described in any other language: it has to be translated into symbol, myth, poetry. However we put it, man has this unconquerable memory of some original harmony and unity, some primal innocence in creation, against which he measures and evaluates its present disorder. And when I say creation I mean the *whole* of creation. God is not only interested in our species. The whole creation is the object of his everlasting love: 'Are not two sparrows sold for a farthing? and not one of them shall fall on the ground without your Father'.[1] God cares for the sparrows and the flowers and the rivers and the lonely deserts. Creation is the object of his love. But Bishop Heber was wrong when he wrote that 'every prospect pleases, and only man is vile'. There is a great deal of misery and meaningless suffering in the natural creation, and it can't all be laid at man's door.

> . . . the suffering of innocent nature, the imperfection and corruption that penetrates all life . . . the horrors of inherited insanity, mental agonies, the whole economy of disease, especially animal disease, seem to point beyond man to some fundamental disharmony between creation and God.[2]

We are brought, inevitably, to the conclusion that the very stuff and matter of creation, the very materials from which we and all creation are formed, are mysteriously faulty and flawed and no longer adequately fulfil their original purpose —the way faulty design and shoddy material can build danger and accident and tragedy into a bridge or motor-car. It is so hard to put this into any language at all, except the high and tragic utterance of music or poetry, but there is a sense in which we are led to the conclusion that the creation itself has wrenched itself from its original purpose and is rushing heedlessly to some great rendezvous with tragedy. Various theologians have tried to put it into words, and Milton tried to put it into poetry. All talk about a creation almost personal in its relationship with God; a relationship of intimacy and harmony, like the unity between an inspired conductor and his orchestra who, together, create a unity of beauty. And this unity was not the unity of coercion; it was the unity, the true unity, of choice, of partnership, of love.

We only have to say these words to see the awful possibilities they contain, for the choice, to be genuine, must contain the possibility of rejection. The awful seed of freedom contains, in germ, all the misery and evil that has stalked the history of the cosmos. Somehow, in some timeless moment, perhaps before the creation of man, the harmony was broken off by the creation, the partnership with the conductor was repudiated, and the great unity was broken; the music ceased. The creation sought, somehow, to organise itself independently of God. Or, to change the image and bring in another element, it is a bit like a nation which has been invaded by a foreign power which conquers it and sets up an alien tyranny and deposes the rightful ruler. The loyalists, like the old Scottish Jacobites, go underground or take to the hills. They preserve the memory of the authority of their rightful king, but the political reality seems at every turn to deny their loyalty and their hope. Something of the sort has happened. It is not that God's authority and the memory of his love have been completely expunged from his creation—the memory of them is there to haunt us with longing and nostalgia—but his rule is a disguised rule, he is 'God in the heather', as it were, banished from the centres of power, gathering his resistance, making forays into the strongholds that oppose him, but not yet restored to his rightful rule. And this is not just fanciful language. The Bible and our Lord himself are quite certain that there is, in the creation, a personal, satanic opposition to God; a tyranny that sets itself against his rule, and that God, by some mysterious self-limitation, permits it to exist until the creation itself turns it out. I suppose the best analogy is from human parenthood. There comes a time when any parent must limit himself, even at great risk to his child, if his child is to be given the freedom to mature into adulthood. He runs the risk of losing a child in order to gain a friend. Without the risk of freedom there can be no maturity, but the risk is painful and the results can sometimes be tragic. In some such way, the creation, like the prodigal son, has gone into a far country, far from the sorrowing father. But these are all poetic images, ways of attempting to express what cannot be expressed with any real certainty. What seems undeniable is that the creation has separated itself from God and outlawed him, driven him underground, by some massive tragedy of misused freedom.

And this cosmic pattern is repeated in each individual soul.

Each of us misuses his freedom. We repeat, recapitulate in our own experience, that first disobedience and separation from the tender fatherhood of God. We have dethroned him and set up another in his place. Each man has become his own authority, his own ruler, his own judge. We conduct our own little one-man band. And, of course, so does everyone else. So the creation becomes a perfect pandemonium of competing egos, all convinced of their own centrality. A simple physical parallel will make this plain. There is a real sense in which each of us is, physically, the centre of the universe; that is to say, the perspective from which we gaze upon the world is always from the self and its confines. I cannot get out from behind my eyes and see the universe from my neighbour's perspective. *I* am the centre of my universe; it is spread out round *me*. I am the centre of perspective, the focal point of vision. This physical centrality is unavoidable. And it is a parable of that spiritual centrality which is also true, though tragic. Because each of us becomes his own reference-point; we become *self*-centred; signficance is located in our*self;* we become the central fact of our own existence. *And so does every man.* And this is man's tragedy: all those competing ego-centres and colliding selves and conflicting perspectives. Yet none of them is the central point of reference. We cannot, any of us, make music on our own without that central figure to lead us all in harmony and disciplined beauty. We are all locked within the confines of our egos. And this accounts for that vexing paradox that afflicts us. We have a vague and tantalising memory of the rightful ruler and the proper harmony, but at the same time we have this well-nigh ungovernable urge to go on doing things in our own way, to be our own centre.

Perhaps an illustration from the study of abnormal psychology will make this clearer. We know a great deal today about the phenomenon known as 'psychosis'.

> A psychosis is a mental illness in which the patient fails to discriminate between stimuli arising within himself and stimuli received from the external world. The healthy personality accurately perceives and evaluates the environment. When the stress of conflict between the self and the environment becomes too great, however, the perceptive and evaluative functions of the personality may break down. In such situations the person appears to distort his concept of the environment into a form which is more satisfactory for him; he organises it into a less confusing place in order to protect himself. In the process he loses contact with reality and becomes psychotic.[3]

Related to the phenomenon of psychosis is the intensely difficult problem of 'autism', particularly in children. The word is derived from the Greek word for 'self' and, as the term suggests, is used to describe a particularly tragic imprisoning of the child totally within the self, so that it is unable to relate to or receive authentic messages from others. As far as the condition is understood, it seems to consist of a pathological inability to apprehend and be in touch with external reality. The subject is thus locked up within the confines of the self, sealed off from any effective contact with other selves, receiving only very faulty and garbled signals from those outside. In caring for autistic children, an almost superhuman patience and understanding is called for, and parents who have written on the subject frequently describe their relationship with their autistic children, whom they deeply love yet feel mysteriously cut-off from, as 'crucifying'. The word and its allusions are significant and I shall return to the theme in a later chapter. For the moment I wish only to note two things: first of all, there is a continuity between our own normal self-centredness and that pathological heightening of it we call psychosis or even autism. We are all, to a greater or less degree, locked off from others and from Transcendent Reality. Secondly, ours is an autistic universe, mysteriously separated from our proper environment, receiving only very faulty and garbled signals from that Transcendence which gave us life and calls to us. We are cut off from our Father, immured within the narrow confines of our own egos, yet tortured by rumours and remembrances of a former joy and communion. This is man's tragedy, and he is incapable of overcoming it by his own efforts. By definition, the self *is* the problem, and the self is unable to help itself. 'Wretched man that I am, who will deliver me from this prison?'[4] This is the fundamental predicament of man. How is he delivered from it?

The Christian tradition has seen and experienced the answer to that problem in the person and teaching of Jesus Christ. Because of what he achieved and because of what he meant to those who had experienced liberation through him, it was very soon strongly felt that his appearance and his coming among men was no accident of birth. *His* coming, unlike all others, was a direct initiative of God; it was part of the 'determinate counsel and foreknowledge of God'[5]; it was not the consequence of the will or action of man, but of God.[6] In Christ God, like the loving father of an autistic son, had taken dramatic and costly action to redeem the tragic bondage of his children and break down the psychic barrier between them. In Christ God was reconciling the world unto himself again,[7] was slowly prising us away from our fatal self-preoccupation to an awareness of his glorious and enriching and life-giving Reality.

As I said in the last chapter, Christ achieved this by what he said and by what he was and did. First of all, then, by what he *said*. Christ showed men what they were and what God was. In a series of dramatic and explosive teaching devices and encounters, he opened to men their own true situation and the true nature of God which their own autistic perceptions had distorted. His teaching strategy was twofold. First of all, he exposed men with ruthless and punishing clarity to the true nature of their predicament. *Then* he opened to them the majestic tenderness and everlasting love of the accepting Father. He stripped the ego bare, allowing it nothing with which to boast, and then showed it that its only true and certain hope lay in the Father's love. A parable will exemplify the first part of the strategy, and an encounter the second. The parable is about the two men who went up into the Temple to pray, the one a Pharisee and the other a Tax Collector.

> Two men went up into the temple to pray; the one a Pharisee, and the other a publican. The Pharisee stood and prayed thus with himself, God, I thank thee, that I am not as other men are, extortioners, unjust, adulterers, or even as this publican. I fast twice in the week, I give tithes of all that I possess.
>
> And the Publican, standing afar off, would not lift up so much as his eyes unto heaven, but smote upon his breast, saying, God, be merciful to me a sinner.
>
> I tell you, this man went down to his house justified rather than the other. (Luke 18.10–14.)

It is almost impossible to understand the real meaning of this parable today. Almost anyone who reads it thinks he gets the meaning straight away. On the one hand you have the hypocrite, boasting of his piety; and on the other hand you have the humble little tax collector begging for forgiveness. It is obvious whose side the reader is on, and, thinks he, the point of the parable is obvious. The reader is almost certainly wrong in his first interpretation of this apparently moralistic little tale. In fact, this is not a simple little parable at all. It is not one of those homely little yarns which we like to think Jesus spun from his inexhaustible fund of peasant wisdom. This parable, like most of our Lord's parables, is a *word-weapon.* It is not meant to lull our superficial prejudices; it is meant to blow up in our faces like a letter-bomb. The only way to hear it is to hear it with all the affronted surprise of its first audience.

First of all, then, there is the Pharisee. The very word ruins the story for us. We think we know what a pharisee is: he's the pious hypocrite, the cartoon Christian. But that is not how Jesus' listeners would have heard the word. In the first place, the Pharisee in this story was not a hypocrite. A hypocrite is an actor, a sham, a man who covers up cynicism with a cloak of piety. This man's religion was no sham. He was a genuine and saintly leader of the Jewish church. While, doubtless, there were hypocritical Pharisees, the Pharisees as a whole were respected as a group of people who took their religion seriously and were genuinely committed to the worship of God and the keeping of his law. The word today is almost synonomous with hypocrite. This is not how Jesus' listeners would have understood it. And the Pharisee in this parable was even better than most. The Jewish law required the Jew to fast *one day a year* in repentance for their sins. The man in the parable fasted *twice a week.* This meant that he gave up food and drink from sunrise till sunset. A fast like this in the heat of the East is a great act of self-denial. This man fasted for the sins of his people. His religion was no hypocrisy. It hurt. It meant an empty belly and a parched throat. This Pharisee's religion meant something. But more, even, than that. The Jew had to pay certain taxes: he had to pay a Temple tax every year, and in addition to that he had to pay a sort of religious purchase tax on everything he bought. He had to pay what the parable calls a tithe. On certain items this tithe or tax was deducted at source from the producer. Corn, new wine and oil were all taxed at source, so Jews did not have to pay tithe on these items when they bought them in the market (though doubtless the producer clawed back some of the tithe by a proportionate loading of the price). The Pharisee in the parable, however, insisted on tithing even these. He made great economic sacrifices for the glory and service of God. Who of us can say that this man's religion was a sham? Unlike most of us to whom religion is a peripheral matter which is never allowed to impede our pleasures or seriously hurt our purses, this man's religion was a rugged exercise in constant self-denial. And there is something else to note. The man in the parable did not claim any glory for himself in all that he did. *He thanked God* for the privilege of serving him, for the opportunity of giving away half his income. And when he thanked God for not making him like certain other men, he was not necessarily boasting. As far as he was concerned, his vocation was a gift. He thanked God for keeping him from sin, and calling him to a life of dedication. Is this wrong?

Jesus' listeners would be in no doubt. As far as they were concerned Jesus, in his picture of the Pharisee, had described a saint, the kind of man they most admired.

The tax collector was a different matter. Tax collectors or publicans were not mousy, wee men from the Inland Revenue, doing a necessary if unpopular job. Tax collectors were two things—they were traitors and quislings, and they were thieves. The Roman Empire had an ingenious way of collecting taxes. When it took over a country, as it had taken over Palestine, it imposed a tax or levy on the inhabitants, but it did not bother to collect the tax itself. It subcontracted the job to tax-farmers, as they were called. These were strong-arm men who collected the taxes in a certain area and passed them back to Rome, having, in the process, taken a substantial cut for themselves. They used murder and coercion to collect taxes and were the most hated men in their native lands, hated because they co-operated with the enemy in oppressing their own people for financial gain. The very word tax collector would have an immediate effect on a first-century Jew, just as the word quisling or Nazi had an immediate effect on the British during the Second World War. It was almost impossible for a tax collector to receive forgiveness in the eyes of a Jew. Sorrow was not enough. A visible and effective penance was necessary: he had to give up his profession and restore all that he had embezzled in full, plus a fifth. How could he do this? He'd bullied and defrauded thousands in his lifetime: how could he possibly make restitution? He is reduced to an entirely appropriate despair: 'God, be merciful to me a sinner.' We must banish from our mind the sympathetic vision of a humble little clerk, beating his breast over a few private vices. Jesus was talking about a really desperate and evil character.

Jesus' listeners would be in no doubt about which of these men was right or justified in God's eyes: a saint and benefactor of society on the one hand, and a gangster and parasite upon his people on the other. Pope John or Al Capone—the choice is obvious, isn't it? They must have drawn in their breath in disbelief at his last words: 'The tax collector went down to his house justified rather than the other.' What can it possibly mean? It cannot, obviously, mean that Jesus approved of screwing money out of poor farmers and disapproved of fasting and the giving of alms. It obviously can't mean that he approved, in principle, of the activities of the tax collector and disapproved, in principle, of men who were trying to be holy. The main point in this parable is very subtle and fundamental to Jesus' whole teaching. It is repeated in an even more outrageous form in the parable of the labourers in the vineyard. In that parable Jesus described the extraordinary behaviour of a vineyard-owner who hired men at different times throughout a long, hot day. In defiance of every canon of distributive justice he gave them all the same wage: a penny to those who had laboured the whole day and a penny to those who had laboured but one hour. The scandalous point which Jesus is making in both parables is that man's selfishness is so radical that even his highest activity, his most idealistic behaviour, is still self-centred. His holiness is only a more refined selfishness and, therefore, a more dangerous selfishness, for it can lull him into ignorance of his true state. Even the dedicated practice of a heroic faith leads man to a more subtle form of autism or 'self-ism'. His long hot day in the vineyard traps him into the conviction that he has, somehow, earned by his own efforts a right relationship with God. This is the higher selfishness, Jesus claimed, and he reserved for it his most scorching words.

It is a mistake to popularise or liberalise Christ's ferocity here, to read into his denunciation of religion a sort of modern humanism. He was not denying the moral integrity of the religious leaders of his day in favour of a sentimental advocacy of colourful vice. He was not, by a wilful perversion of justice, claiming that obvious sinners were better than obvious saints. He was not denying that some had laboured all day and others for an hour. He *was* saying that, measured by the reality of the holiness and centrality of God, it was *all* beside the point! Man, as such, was chained to his own ego, and even his highest and best pursuits were tragic manifestations of that state of radical bondage to the self.

The danger of religion—and it is a perennial danger—is that it can lull a man into a complacent forgetfulness of his true condition. Jesus attacked the noblest exponents of the noblest religion of his day for the simple reason that their very nobility was their greatest danger! So profound and subtle was man's disease that it rooted most firmly in the highest form of the human organism. He tackled the religious leaders of Judaism, not because he had the shallow modernist's contempt for their zeal, but because he loved them, probably above all others, and knew the great risks they ran. He knew that there was no blindness blinder than the blindness of the genuinely good, no autism more radical than the autism of the saint. The only advantage which the publican had was the knowledge of his own profound hopelessness. Measured by any standard, he was a complete failure; he had nothing at all to which he could cling to protect him from himself; he was totally broken down and lost. There was no hope anywhere and so he was thrust towards a radical recognition of the true human situation. Only in God had he the slightest chance. There was no special pleading, no refined selfishness, no shred of self-respect left at all. He was faced of a sudden with the awful clarity of his true condition. And, said Jesus, the publican's approach was the only valid human approach. By one of those strange paradoxes of which God is so fond, the sinner teaches the saint how to approach God—with total and despairing abandon. Only God can save us. There is nothing human to which we can cling. Yet the piercing despair of the tax collector cuts through all obstacles, straight to the heart of God: 'God, be merciful to me a sinner.'

In parable after parable and encounter after encounter Jesus demonstrated his profound knowledge of the human condition: 'Jesus knew all men, and needed not that any should testify of man: for he knew what was in man'.[8] He saw through man with a piercing realism which located the source of man's tragedy in his chronic egotism, an egotism which infected all his institutions, both noble and vile. But he sought to address himself to man at his most confident and compelling, for then he was likely to be furthest from that radical self-knowledge which was the necessary prelude to his Gospel of God's love. Man's need was God's opportunity, but that opportunity was wasted if man remained unaware of his need, locked up in his own self-confidence. Hence the paradox of his ferocious attack upon the traditions and disciplines of the Pharisees.

This profound realism about man is poles apart from the modern liberal view of man which sees the disorders of man and society as created by faulty structures and institutions. This modern version of Pharisaism, which is endemic in our technocratic society, sees the solution to the human predicament in a purely functional adjustment of human structures and institutions. It is an approach which currently dominates much of the thinking behind ecclesiastical reform. Given that initial premise of human tragedy as functional disorder, the argument of the modern Pharisee is formidable. No matter where you start in your choice of human structures, you can make a compelling case for reform or revolution since, by definition, they are all faulty or corrupt. The nation-state is an obvious example. So is the university or the Church or the nuclear family. All are susceptible to this approach, for all are more or less corrupt. Though this functional, humanistic approach to human disorder is far from new, it has received massive new support from the emergence of modern technological society and its discipline of clinical objectivity.

The most significant new phenomenon in our culture has been the emergence of the technical expert. The success of the scientific method in dealing with the control of man's natural environment has consecrated the technical expert as the high-priest or super-pharisee of our era. The expert deals with the pure objectivity of data: everything, as we have seen, is Out-There waiting to be manipulated and rearranged into patterns of his choice. The successes of this method in dealing, for instance, with the vast technical achievement of landing men on the moon are spectacular. But the expert makes a fateful and subtle leap in his argument: he applies the objective method to the field of human relations, or tries to. And here he comes unstuck, or will soon, for human beings are intractable, irrational, and there is a fundamental recalcitrancy which is built in to the human situation. Human beings will not, for long, respond with the same gratifying precision to expert manipulation as do more objective data. But the myth persists and has thrown up a whole new science of social engineering. Given the right programme, we are told, the irritating malfunctions which presently upset the proper performance of Project Man will be banished once and for all. At this very moment the experts are working on it somewhere. The enormous American 'think-tank', the Rand Corporation, for example, is at this moment engaged in a search for the solution to the problems that presently beset mankind. There is a lunatic clarity about this approach, if you accept the basic premise, though one wonders why the premise is never questioned, why the fundamental question is never asked: 'Why do all of man's institutions, even his highest, inevitably become corrupt?' The only answer to that question is that man himself is intrinsically faulty and corrupt by definition; it is the *humanity factor itself* which is intractable. The problems which beset man do not reside in faulty structures and institutions but in his own nature. The virus of man's self-regard will soon infect any brave new utopia which he constructs. Man's disease is chronic and it infects the very thought processes of the experts and idealists who work to find its cure, ensuring that all his projects have this built-in, ontological flaw. Man cannot save himself. How can he? since it is his own nature which afflicts him.

> For what else is man's misery but his own disobedience to himself, so that in consequence of his not being willing to do what he could do, he now wills to do what he cannot? . . . For who can count how many things he wishes which he cannot do, so long as he is disobedient to himself, that is so long as his mind and his flesh do not obey his will.[9]

But this is not the whole truth about man as declared by Christ. The fact that he called men to an awareness of their true condition is clear proof that there was more in man than chronic egotism. As well as being tied and bound to his fallen nature, man is also able to transcend it; he is able to bring his self-interest under the discipline of a higher law than his own desire; he is capable of partial conformity to an ideal. If Christ's realism corresponded to his profound awareness of the reality of the Fall of Man, the demand he made upon men, the challenge he put to them corresponds to another great theme in the Biblical tradition, the doctrine of Creation. According to this view man is created in the image of God, and he is created good; this is the primary fact from which all other facts proceed. It is true that creation has been corrupted, but even this is a negative witness to the primary fact. But Creation is not to be thought of as a single act of God in the past, like the throwing of an electric switch; Creation is a permanent activity of God who is ever at work in his universe, ordering and sustaining it. 'My Father worketh hitherto, and I work.'[10] When man struggles in the world to bring good out of evil and order out of chaos, he is working with God who is endlessly engaged in the task of restoring his Creation to its original purpose. The world is still the arena of God's creative activity, and man is called to be a fellow-worker with God in the task of restoring his damaged creation. This accounts for man's strange passion for righteousness in a world of complicated oppressions and injustices. There is something about the very nature of reality which impels men to seek righteousness. According to Biblical religion, this is the action of God in the souls of men.

Man is caught, therefore, in the midst of this strange duality of self-regard and self-transcendence, and he is unable to lift himself out of the tragic predicament of his own nature. He is an essentially tragic creature, constitutionally driven to seek ideals which he is constitutionally incapable of realising. He is engaged in an endless search for something which endlessly eludes his grasp. None of his achievements is ever completely innocent of evil or completely devoid of good. It is this which gives man's history its tragic dimension: it is this which accounts for the grandeur and the misery of man.

Jesus' whole ministry was a gigantic effort to get men to realise their true condition and the desperate plight they were in. By word and action he called men to a radical re-estimation of their status. His parables were weapons aimed at the self-righteous and self-confident. He was intent upon blasting through the armour-plated egos of the 'good' and the clever, to expose them to their own poverty and corruption and radical need for God. His actions had the same intent. He conspicuously associated with the despised classes, the outcasts and sinners. To them he offered the certainty of God's acceptance because they, of all men, knew their true status, knew that there was nothing human in which they could trust, no boast they could make. Like the tax collector in the parable, they knew that they offended against every ethical and religious canon. They were the 'poor', dependent utterly upon the charity of God. They had no 'riches' of their own, nothing which they could trust, no alternative to God. They were thrust back on him alone. His association with the outcast and sinner, therefore, was itself an action-parable, and it gave even greater offence to the self-confident autism of his day than did his purely verbal offensive. By word and example he seemed intent upon destroying the whole edifice of religious and social self-confidence.

That he called the poor and not the righteous was apparently the dissolution of all ethics; it seemed as if moral conduct meant nothing in God's eyes. The world around Jesus based man's relationship with God on his moral conduct. Because the gospel did not do that, it shook religion to its foundations. Thus the stumbling block arose from the good news—and not primarily from Jesus' call to repentance. The message that God wanted dealings with the sinners, and that they were nearer to God than the righteous, provoked a passionate protest from the Pharisees. At every turn Jesus was compelled to give an answer to the offence taken by the Pharisees to the gospel. He did this above all in the form of parables. The parables which deal with the reprieving of sinners are not a presentation but a *vindication of the good news*.[11]

And this is still the main offence of the gospel. Men will not admit their poverty and helplessness. Like the rich fool in another parable, their self-confidence, fundamentally precarious though it is, is welded round their psyche like an armoured shell. This is true above all of the rich and self-confident technocratic culture of the West. We have, by our own brilliance, built our barns and harvested our grain, and we rest heavily upon that fragile security: 'thou hast much goods laid up for many years; take thine ease, eat, drink, and be merry.'[12] The unquestioned self-confidence of our culture has permeated every aspect of our lives, smothering the very challenge of faith with an amused and unconcerned dismissal. This very pathology was itself fortified by a recent trend in theology which maintained that man has now 'come of age', and could, henceforth, live 'as if there were no God', relaxed and confident in his own power. The virile realism of Christ was replaced by a facile optimism about man which appealed to him 'in his strength'. The trend, like all trends, has died a natural death, but not before it had effected an enduring distortion in much contemporary theology. This was never Christ's way. He did not appeal to men in their strength and self-confidence; he tried to bring them to an awareness of their weakness and need and profound poverty. The essential prelude to the glorious liberation of the gospel is that piercing cry of the tax-collector: 'God be merciful unto me a sinner.'

8

The Accepting Father

I SAID in Chapter seven that Christ's teaching strategy was twofold. First of all, he exposed men with ruthless and punishing clarity to the true nature of their autistic predicament; then he opened to them the majestic tenderness and everlasting love of the accepting Father. He stripped the ego bare, allowing it nothing with which to boast and then showed it that its only real security lay in the everlasting certainty of the Father's love. I want to try to demonstrate the second part of the teaching strategy in this chapter by an examination and interpretation of the account which we find in John's Gospel of the woman who was caught in the act of adultery and brought to Jesus by her accusers. This passage raises profound questions about the meaning and consequences of human law and our Lord's attitude towards it, and it makes an appropriate prelude to an examination of the Passion which was our Lord's final 'action parable' and gathers together the whole meaning of his earthly life.

The account of our Lord's encounter with the adulterous woman, though it is found in our bibles at the beginning of the eighth chapter of John's gospel, is generally held to be a 'floating pericope' which is more in the style of the Synoptics than of John. While its exact provenance is of little importance, its meaning is of crucial importance to an understanding of Christ's teaching about God.

> The scribes and Pharisees brought unto him a woman taken in adultery; and when they had set her in the midst, they say unto him, Master, this woman was taken in adultery, in the very act. Now Moses in the law commanded us, that such should be stoned: but what sayest thou? This they said, tempting him, that they might have to accuse him. But Jesus stooped down, and with his finger wrote on the ground, as though he heard them not. So when they continued asking him, he lifted up himself, and said unto them, He that is without sin among you, let him first cast a stone at her. And again he stooped down and wrote on the ground. And they which heard it, being convicted by their own conscience, went out one by one, beginning at the eldest, even unto the last: and Jesus was left alone, and the woman standing in the midst. When Jesus had lifted up himself, and saw none but the woman, he said unto her, Woman, where are those thine accusers? hath no man condemned thee? She said, No man, Lord. And Jesus said unto her, Neither do I condemn thee: go, and sin no more.
> (John 8.3–11)

It is important to understand the exact meaning of this event. It was meant to be an execution. When the scribes and Pharisees said that the adulteress was to be stoned, according to their law, they did not intend to pick up a few stones and shoo her away, the way we should chase off a dog which was barking at our heels. They meant something much grimmer: they meant to pelt her with stones till she was dead. The Jews took a very serious view of adultery. A verse in the book of Leviticus says that the adulterer and the adulteress 'shall surely be put to death'; and the book of Deuteronomy lays down that the death is to be by stoning. In a later version of the Jewish law the penalty for adultery is given as strangulation, and even the method of strangulation is laid down with considerable detail. The man is to be enclosed in dung up to his knees, and a soft towel set within a rough towel is to be placed around his neck. Then one executioner is to draw the towel in one direction while the other draws it in the other direction, 'until he be dead'. Jesus was being invited to preside at an execution.

As with the parable of the Pharisee and the Tax Collector, it is almost impossible for us to feel the full impact of this event. On the face of it, it is an absurd story, but we have so sentimentalised Jesus and we think so little of adultery today, that we cannot really hear the story in all its scandalous absurdity. It does not shock us in the appropriate way. We simply cheer unthinkingly, because once again good old liberal Jesus has routed those appallingly conservative and hypocritical Pharisees. And that is to miss the authentic scandal of this narrative. Let me try to bring it up to date in a modern paraphrase.

> A certain man was caught raping a girl, in the very act, and he was brought before judge and jury for trial. The jury filed in to hear the evidence, which conclusively proved the guilt of the rapist. Before leaving the court to consider their verdict, the judge leant over the bar to address the jury. 'Ladies and gentlemen of the jury', he said to them, 'before you start to consider your verdict in this case, I wish to give you one instruction. You may only find this man guilty if you yourself have never been guilty of harbouring lustful thoughts in your minds.' Slightly embarrassed, the jury filed out to examine their consciences and reach a verdict. One by one they disqualified themselves. When there was no one left except the judge and the rapist, the judge turned to him and said: 'Has no one found you guilty?' 'No one, my Lord,' he replied. 'Neither do I', said, the judge, 'go, and commit no more crimes.'

Imagine the reaction on the following day: the petitions, the marches, the protests of irate parents of teen-age daughters. That judge would be hastily removed, the case would be re-tried, and the rapist would be sent up for five years. And quite right too.

Adultery to the Jew was one of the deadliest of sins and one of the most harshly punished crimes. He felt for it the loathing we feel for rape. The Jew knew that adultery hit at the very roots of society. If tolerated, it would lead to moral and social chaos. Hence the enormity of what Jesus did. And we must not think of him as engaged in reforming the criminal and moral law. No one today would agree with capital punishment for adultery, but that is not the point. Jesus, in this event and in many others, took an axe to the roots of human justice. He was not out to reform *Jewish* law; he seemed intent on banishing *all* law! Aggressors were not to be resisted. If they move in on you and take over your town and rape your daughters, you don't, according to Jesus, do the commonsense thing, which is to resist them by force—you bless them, you turn the other cheek. If a man steals your jewellery, you don't, according to Jesus, phone the police—you run after him and tell him he forgot the silver. What can it possibly all mean? We have so sentimentalised Jesus that we have lost all sense of the enormity of what he said and did. Perhaps it takes a Jewish theologian to grasp the full scandal of his conduct.

> For civil justice he substituted the command to nonresistance, which must result in the loss of all social order; the social regulation and protection of family life he replaced with the prohibition of all divorce, and with praise of those who 'made themselves eunuchs for the kingdom of heaven's sake'; instead

> of manifesting interest in labour, in economic and political achievement, he recommended the unanxious, toilless life exemplified by birds and lilies; he ignored even the requirements of ordinary distributive justice when he said, 'Man, who has made me a judge or divider over you' . . . Jesus ignored everything concerned with material civilisation.[1]

One thing is certain: sinful, autistic man *needs* the law to protect himself from himself. We know that men, including ourselves, are evil and lustful, and so we have to protect society, we have to protect ourselves against ourselves if we are not to slide into a murderous anarchy in which evil knows no restraint and wickedness no punishment. Because of the radical egotism of his nature, man has had to evolve the protective sanctions of law as a hedge against the worst excesses of his own nature. This was certainly the view held by Paul. He tells us that lawful authority is constituted by God for the protection of the innocent and the punishment of the wicked. He says: 'If you would avoid being alarmed at the government authorities, lead an honest life and you will be commended by it . . . But if you do wrong, you may well be alarmed; a magistrate does not wield the power of the sword for nothing, he is God's servant for the infliction of divine vengeance upon evildoers'.[2] Paul was very realistic about human nature. He knew what is all too obvious, that civilisation is a thin skin stretched tightly over a terrible darkness, and law is one of the ways in which we keep the skin intact. We may all be potential rapists in our hearts, but that knowledge cannot hinder us from gaoling those who are rapists in fact. And on the face of the tangled and tragic history of human civilisation who can doubt that Paul is right? On the one hand we must go on building righteousness, inch by slow inch, but, on the other hand, we must recognise the ineradicable nature of human selfishness and protect ourselves against it. We must build protections against the evil that is constantly in our midst. For instance, it will never be enough to exhort men not to practise racial or sexual discrimination; we must make laws that will punish them if they do, in order to protect those who are their victims. Sadly, it is also true that it will never be enough to exhort men to live at peace with one another unless we are able to support our exhortation with force where necessary. By these means we may be able to create a context within which men may grow towards righteousness, but righteousness is never anything we will possess absolutely in this life. We must be like the children of Israel when they rebuilt the walls of Jerusalem under the direction of Nehemiah:

> They that builded the wall and they that bare burdens laded themselves, everyone with one of his hands wrought in the work, and with the other held his weapon; and the builders, every one had his sword girded by his side, and so he builded.[3]

It is the great glory of the Jewish religion that it acted as the lawmaker for mankind. It recognised the central importance of law for the human community. In building the walls of civilisation, it taught man to gird himself with the protection of law if he wished to preserve his fragile security. This was and is one of the greatest achievements of the Jewish spirit. Yet here comes Jesus Christ to destroy the fragile control of law over human evil by rejecting the fundamental distinction between thought and action and by, apparently, encouraging us to allow evil to go unchecked and unpunished. What can it possibly mean?

This is a paradox which has baffled and taxed the mind of the Church for 2000 years. Individual Christians and groups of Christians have resolved the paradox for themselves by adopting one interpretation and sticking to it. Whole communities of Christians have allowed themselves to be massacred unresisting for the sake of their fidelity to what they took to be an explicit command from Jesus Christ to renounce the protections of natural justice. Others, equally sincere, have taken up arms against notorious evil and aggression in the name of the same Christ, and have given their lives in battle. No one interpretation of the paradox has had universal appeal. Must we leave the matter there, stuck in the midst of an irresolvable dilemma, or is there some ground on which we can come together? I think there is. I think that Jesus, by these mysterious and demanding sayings and encounters, was opening up for us the very heart of God. I believe that we need the law to protect ourselves from ourselves. But there is a desperate sadness in that fact, and it has awful consequences. One of them is that human law, in its widest sense, is often corrupted by the very conditions that make its existence necessary: it becomes a blunt instrument which easily becomes the evil it set out to oppose. Men have committed great crimes in the name of law. Throughout history men and nations have created a desert and called it peace.

But there is another and more awful consequence of the necessity of law. So important is law to man, that he has used it as a model for interpreting the meaning of the universe and the nature of God. By an obvious process of projection, man has seen God as Judge, and the effect of that projection has been terrible beyond all words. By this simple means man has depersonalised his relationship with God and has, instead, interpreted and understood it in terms of system and law—with profound effects. We all know how guilty we are of innumerable sins. When a judge considers what to do with a criminal convicted of a crime, he takes the accused's previous record into account. If the man has 490 previous convictions for assault, he is unlikely to let him go free for the 491st offence, because his primary function is to protect society. He cannot only think of the criminal. His record is held against him. Law, as I said, is so important to us that it affects our thinking about everything, including God. So we come to think of God as judge, poring over our record. Everything we do, so we imagine, is recorded in a celestial IBM computer. I know that I am sometimes paralysed by guilt over a particular sin I have committed for the 500th time. I think of my record, stretching back down the years, stamped with failure and sin, smudged with ineffectual regret, and I see God sternly assessing my guilt and weighing my punishment, checking that little card punched full of poignant little holes. And how many of us bear the burden of our sins like that! And they are a burden, because we are unable to mend our ways *or* still our consciences. In some cases, guilt of this sort can become a real disease of the soul and mind, reducing men and women to anguished wrecks. And all because we see the universe as a vast legal system in which a close check is kept on our record.

And it is this to which Jesus took an axe! He said in so many words: 'It may be true that society has to protect itself against you, but my Father doesn't. He is a loving Father; the news he wishes you to hear is that nothing you do can separate you from his love. He stretches forth his hands towards you every day, not in judgement and condemnation, but to draw you to himself. He has, for you, an everlasting love. You may smite him on the cheek—he will turn the other. You may curse and deny him—he will bless you. You may rob and despoil him—he will heap greater riches upon you. You can never escape from or kill his love for you; it will follow you down the years, unjudging, tender, full of pity and stronger than death. It will die for you. That is the good news.' It turns the world's values and standards upside down. It opens up to us the vision of an unbelievable love. It lies at the centre of all those heart-wrenching riddles Jesus spoke to us.

On one level this might appear to deepen man's despair: faced with the intolerable graciousness of God's love and the knowledge of his own moral impotence, what is man to do? He is scarcely capable of un-selfregarding love towards those whom he is bound to by the ties of birth and natural affection, and he seems to be totally incapable of it at all on a collective level, where he is moved by forces he can neither entirely understand nor control. Of what use is this sublime knowledge? The point is that it is of no *use* to man at all. It cannot be used as an instrument for any of man's purposes, since it is the very ground that makes his purposes possible in the first place. It can only be accepted, said 'yes' to. It is always a gift. But it should give him a fundamental security in the face of the tragedies of existence. It is a well-known psychological fact that ability to love is the result of first being loved. Only the child brought up in the original security of love can really develop the mature ability to love others in return. Reinhold Niebuhr puts it this way:

> The capacity of the self to relate itself to others cannot be achieved by a robust moral will. It is a gift of the original security of the self; that is, it is a matter of 'grace'.[4]

Only when men can relax in the knowledge that they are secure in the love of the Father can they in turn find the courage to love in return: 'We love him, because he first loved us.' And the Father's love is always before our love, and continues during our love's failures. One of the consequences of this knowledge is that it releases men to live bravely in a tragic world, in spite of their mistakes, and in spite of the intractable nature of their sinfulness. It gives men the security to take risks.

In his teaching about sin, Jesus revealed himself as having a profound psychological knowledge of man. 'He knew what was in man.' Man's tragedy is that he is made for God, yet he is imprisoned within himself. He cannot effect his own liberation, since he is, at the same time, prisoner, prison, and prison-guard. Release comes when interest and attention is transferred from the self to God. This transfer of interest and attention, this revolution within the self, is what Christ meant by 'redemption', since it is, precisely, a profound act or activity of liberation. As we have seen, the essential prelude to this redemption is that stark and tragic awareness of our bondage to the self, which he demanded. The next movement in the act of redemption was a profound shift in our consciousness of the meaning of sin, involving a radical reversal of our usual ideas. Sin is much more than a result or consequence of our radical egotism. Our very awareness and interpretation of sin itself is an expression of that profound autism which characterises us. Guilt, in particular, is a profound expression of our egotism, since it persuades us that we can separate ourselves from God.

This is the final and most chronic symptom of the diseased ego: it arrogates to itself a power that is stronger than God, since it persuades itself that in this way it can lock God out. Guilt is the most chronic symptom of that autism which afflicts man. But Jesus will allow it only the power of self-delusion. He refuses to accept the law and its demands as a model for the tender fatherhood of God. God will not be kept at a distance by the diseased scheming of the self. In one of his most famous parables (which we, in our human-centred way, call the Parable of the Prodigal Son, but which I'm sure he thought of as the Parable of the Accepting Father), he gives us a picture of utterly imperturbable love, going out to meet man, rejoicing. Of course Jesus did not teach that our liberation from the self was effected by a simple recognition of the Father's unconquerable love. There was no automatic trigger mechanism in the human psyche which suddenly switched attention from the self to God. He called men to a life of effort and endurance; he called upon them to enter a revolutionary discipline of self-denial and divine-affirmation. And, of course, he still does, but the ground and motive of this way of life is a profound and releasing shift in awareness which we can only receive as a gift, and which mysteriously empowers us for the struggle.

To put it very simply, it consists of an awareness that God does not punish us for sin, but that sin is its own punishment, since it contrives to keep us from our proper awareness of God. Sin, in essence, is self-fixation, self-pleasing. God does not say: 'If you please yourself I will punish you.' He says: 'My children, there is no happiness or lasting satisfaction in pleasing self. You can only find peace and joy in living in love and harmony with my will, which is your peace. The longer you go on fixing your attention on the self, the longer you postpone your truest joy, and the more difficult you make the adjustment to me you must make one day.' There is a profound difference in the mood of these statements. When we think of sin as breaking the law, we think of God as being against us, and that colours our whole attitude towards him; it fills us with fear and guilt, and that, in turn, only entrenches sin deeper within us. But when we realise that God is not against us but for us, and that he wants us to stop sinning not because it offends him but because it damages *us*, then it can change our whole attitude. No longer paralysed by guilt, we see sin and the struggle against it as something objective, like a hill to be climbed or a job to be done. Its terrors have gone, and its fascination is considerably reduced.

When all this is recognised, we are still faced with the ongoing necessity of denying the self, and this still involves painful discipline, what the old books on the spiritual life called 'mortification'. Evelyn Underhill said that mortification was simply the name we give to those inevitable changes which we must undergo in the transfer of interest from the self to God. But, as always, the way we look at the process is all-important. If you have confined yourself to an easy chair in a musty, darkened room for years, and someone persuades you to forsake it and venture out into the sunlit garden and perhaps, later on, to the hills beyond, the effort will be enormously painful, and if you concentrate all your attention on the pain then you'll never do it. If you say: 'He wanted me to leave this comfy old chair, and straighten out these legs that have been bent for years (the cramp was *indescribable*), and risk my weak old eyes on that harsh sunlight, damned sadist that he is', then you'll never do it. But if you say: 'He wanted me to get out into the fresh air and feel the wind and see the bluebells in the garden; and then he wanted me to go with him to that hill we used to picnic on years ago—but you can imagine the pain in these creaky old legs when I first got out of the chair. Why, I nearly fell and I could only take a few steps at a time—but he kept beckoning me on out into the sunlight, and I'm so glad he made me do it'. Do you see the difference? It all seems the same; the outward action is alike, but the motive and meaning of the action is completely different. Through Christ, God called men to embark on a great journey away from the self and towards him. To make the journey at all we must undergo changes, but we'll never even start if we focus our attention on them. But if we fix it on him and the joy he promises, then we'll find the strength to make the changes, and the humour and gladness to endure them.

It is this daring and revolutionary reversal of man's most carefully developed ideas of God and his demands which marks the uniqueness of Christ's teaching. No *man* could have contrived this totally unexpected yet intrinsically compelling description of the attitude of God to man. It was this momentous reversal of man's best insights which scandalised the religious and political establishments of our Lord's day, and led finally to his death. And it is important to understand that it was a reversal of man's *best* insights. Christ was not engaged in a reform of corrupt human institutions. Rabbi Klausner was right when he complained that Christ ignored everything concerned with human civilisation, and that in this sense he did not belong to civilisation. But this was not because he had no interest in man and his vulnerable craving for security (the record is charged with his compassion for man in his purely human need); it was because he knew that all man's institutions were stamped with the inescapable mark of his chronic egotism, including his deepest religious and moral insights. And none of them could serve as a model for understanding the sublime fatherhood of God. *This knowledge had to come from outside man.* It was a vertical intrusion from the beyond, bisecting man's history. It was an utterly underived and transcendent initiative. It was the only really *new* thing man had ever confronted. And it came to man as both judgement and joy.

It came as judgement, because it would allow man no human security of which to boast and in which to trust. It scattered man's confidence in his own power and achievement like chaff, and reduced him to the status of a dependent child. This accounts for that tragic hostility to Christ which increasingly darkens the pages of the New Testament record. It is impossible to account for this hostility on the basis of a narrow reformist interpretation of Christ. He was not just the most distinguished entrant in the liberal or revolutionary martyrology. There are better ways to deal with rebels and reformers than to execute them, and the Establishment of Christ's day knew this as well as any of us. Christ's challenge was deeper and more ultimate than that superficial estimate will allow. There is enormous significance in the fact that it was the best men, the leaders and benefactors of their race, who rose against Jesus and put him to death. It was precisely because he challenged man as *man* that they rose in fury against him. Before an alcoholic or drug addict can be cured of his dependence he must first reach a moment of truth in which he recognises his complete bondage to his habit. He cannot be helped as long as he pretends to himself that he can handle the situation or make a few adjustments here or there. He must, in the language of Alcoholics Anonymous, 'find his gutter,' that point of utter bankruptcy where he recognises with desolate and overwhelming certainty that he is utterly imprisoned within the addictive cycle. Until this point is reached he resists the knowledge of his dependence as a threat to his own manhood, and his fury is fortified by his own inner doubts. Christ presented a challenge to man which exposed him to the fact of his own bondage to the self and offered him release. 'If ye continue in my word, then are ye my disciples indeed; *and ye shall know the truth, and the truth shall make you free.*' (John 8.31–32). The most confident and successful among his critics reacted with entirely predictable anger to this challenge: 'We be Abraham's seed, and were never in bondage to any man: how sayest thou, Ye shall be made free?' (John 8.33).

But to those who could receive it his message came as joy and peace and liberation. To those who had reached the moment of truth, the awareness of man's utter bondage to the Self, Christ's teaching about God came as redemption. We are told that the poor and sinful heard him with joy. They knew and acknowledged their need, so they were filled with good things. But the rich, the *self*-satisfied were sent empty away. Since they acknowledged no need, they could not recognise the good things he offered them. 'How sayest thou, ye shall be free?'

And it is still the same today. The same challenge is presented and provokes the same puzzled and uncomprehending response. In the language of the theologians, until man acknowledges or is made aware of his utter *contingency*, the secondary and derivative nature of his being, he cannot come to a knowledge of and dependence upon the utter and adorable and intrinsic reality of the accepting Father. And this is true at every level of his being. Man's intellectual awareness and interpretation of external reality, for instance, is profoundly stunted and distorted till he acknowledges its autonomy and apartness. Indeed, he never discovers reality at all while it comes to him only through the distorting lens of his own imprisoning egotism. But once he is liberated from the confines of the self, he receives a whole new universe in return. When he dies to the self he rises again to a new and expanding creation of unbearable and turbulent beauty. But man would rather lock himself away from this unpredictable and unexpected universe and settle back into the safe predictability of the Egypt of his bondage. Like all slaves, he is afraid of freedom and its risks, and he turns with the frenzy of shame upon those who would remove his fetters or even acknowledge their existence. 'Then took they up stones to cast at him: but Jesus hid himself, and went out of the temple, going through the midst of them, and so passed by.' (John 8.59)

And all this is equally true on a moral level. Here man is even less able to help himself. Every purely human system of self-culture only succeeds in entrenching and refining that subtle egotism which characterises us. This accounts for that mysteriously repellent aura of virtue, unredeemed by any saving vices, which certain earnest souls carry round with them. I have felt coarse and unclean in such company, constantly tempted to a defiant earthiness. As I try to analyse my attitude to such earnestness and my own ill-fated pursuit of perfection, one characteristic stands out—*carefulness*. Any attempt at self-culture, any moralistic religious or political path, results in a deadening of spontaneity; it leads to a carefully measured set of responses and reactions; in fact, an almost overwhelming *self*-consciousness which totally inhibits the faculty for enjoyment. The poor souls who have trapped themselves in this pattern, watching what they eat or what they say, carefully tuning their political or theological responses to the appropriate stimuli, are never really able to let themselves go; they must always be in control. And for this reason they are dreadfully dull company. It is tragic how boring the worthy can be! I am quite sure our Lord felt this. I am sure he actually enjoyed the company of prostitutes and drunkards and the local racketeers, for at least they knew how to let themselves go, and their enjoyment of the world was an enjoyment of something other than the self. Indeed, it was more; it was a blinded longing for that enjoyment of God which all men crave. This is why our Lord took such a generous view of the so-called sins of the flesh. There was in these excesses a genuine element of joy and forgetting of the self. Sexual ecstasy and the enjoyment of alcohol are, in their way, shadows and prefigurings of that joy which haunts us and draws us to itself. But the sins of the spirit, the sins of the Self, are without either joy or contentment.

The only way in which men have ever really successfully dealt with the pathology of the self is by forgetting about it in an attitude of heart-bursting gratitude to God that he is God, and is such a God as forgives to the uttermost. When a man fixes all his interest upon God and his love, and forgets all about himself, even about his sins, then sin and self are conquered; and not because he tackled sin head on, but because he ignored it, looked upon it as of no account. Then it shrivels up and dies, because sin thrives upon attention: it loves fulminations from the pulpit deploring this and that; it revels in publicity; it adores the anguish and guilt it produces in souls who go over themselves like dogs searching for fleas—any attention will do—and it thrives and grows fat and suffocates the soul. But fix your attention upon God and the laughter and joy of his mercy, and it wilts and fades and vanishes like mist in sunshine. This does not mean that the Christian ceases to confess his sins—he remains a realist about himself—but it has a profound effect upon the way he confesses them. The more the Christian discovers about God, the more aware he becomes of his own unworthiness. But he is not heavy with the knowledge: more important than his admitted unworthiness is the impelling and releasing fact of God's eager and forgiving love. This is why the Church's confessional is not a dour and joyless place, like the bar in a court of law. It is a fount of grace, a stream in a dry land, a place of joy and tenderness, because here the soul is constantly assured and reassured of the endless forgiveness of God, as only those who use this most tender sacrament can testify. It is the sacrament of peace and forgiveness, the sacrament of joy and gladness.

This was the new and beautiful paradox that Christ made known to men: he *personalised* Reality by opening men to the knowledge of the Accepting Father. No longer need man systematise and schematise his relationship with and his approach to Reality. Christ had opened to them the tenderness of Being. All man had to do was to go forth from the confines of the self and enter that joy which had been prepared for him from the foundation of the world. No longer was he to draw back in fear and guilt. Love bade him welcome.

> Love bade me welcome; yet my soul drew back,
> Guilty of dust and sin.
> But quick-eyed Love, observing me grow slack

From my first entrance in,
Drew nearer to me sweetly questioning,
If I lacked anything.

A guest, I answered, *worthy* to be here:
Love said, You shall be he.
I the unkind, ungrateful? Ah, my dear,
I cannot look on thee.
Love took my hand, and smiling did reply,
Who made the eyes but I?

Truth, Lord; but I have *marred* them; let my *shame*
Go where it doth deserve.
And know you not, says Love, 'who bore the blame?
My dear, then I will *serve.*
You must sit down, says Love, *and taste my meat.*
So I did sit and eat.

George Herbert

*My italics.

9

The Substitution

H. L. MENCKEN once said that religion was not a syllogism but a poem. I am sure he was right. The reading of a good poem should lead to a moment of recognition, an experience of revelation, an opening to reality that is deeper than reason though it does not exclude it. The recognition should be intrinsically compelling and self-evidencing in its own right. It is a moment of vision which we simply receive, if we receive it at all. Another aspect of the truth of poetry is that we can return to it again and again for further enrichment and increased awareness. It is not simply a piece of syllogistic information which we master and store in our minds for future use. If a poem is valid and honest it is never dimmed by time or invalidated by further research. This is the major distinction between art and science. Genuine art is never outmoded. Fourteenth-century art is still as true today as it was five hundred years ago, while the science of five hundred years ago is largely outmoded. A genuine poem is something which is intrinsically timeless. This is why we can read the poetry of the Middle Ages for its own sake, though we can only study medieval cosmology *historically*, in order to locate its place in the development of man's scientific understanding. Science must discard as it progresses. The science of today is a cumulative result of the rejection and retention of past research, whereas each genuine work of art stands intact in its own right as a complete statement. The test is by paraphrase. It is possible to distil and paraphrase and give the valid conclusions of a given piece of scientific research. Indeed, the explosion of scientific research in our own era makes this process imperative; hence the emergence of 'data banks' which store up the valid conclusions of science for future use and reference. A true work of art, however, must be experienced totally in its own right. If one paraphrases Shakespeare's *Macbeth*, and reduces it to the story-line and conclusion, one has missed the whole point of the play, since the story is merely the vehicle or form which Shakespeare used in proclaiming the tragic vision. All great art, like all great liturgy, is always contemporary, since it is a permanent opening to the beyond and owes nothing to mere 'up-to-dateness'. Like all awareness, of course, it involves discipline and patience and humility. The humbling thing about all art is that it cannot be translated. You cannot understand an Eliot Quartet by first translating it into a basic paraphrase to get the meaning. It does not work like that. The poem can only work as it is in itself. Translation is destruction. It must be encountered in its stubborn and intrinsic 'otherness' if it is to lead to the moment of recognition.

Christ's teaching about God was poetic rather than syllogistic. He did not give theological lectures in which he argued towards unavoidable conclusions. His method had both the beauty and the stark immediacy of all great art. In a series of teaching encounters he brought men to a point of recognition or rejection. They either perceived that God was like this, or they stopped their offended ears and took up stones to cast at him. There can be no doubt that what he proclaimed about God was the subject either of controversy and offence, or of a heart-swelling joy. His teaching seemed to divide men by a mysterious process of judgement. It is impossible to exaggerate this fact. It obviously puzzled his own followers. Each of the Synoptics has included a tragic and enigmatic utterance of our Lord's which underlines this:

> Then when they were by themselves, his close followers and the twelve asked him about the parables, and he told them: 'The secret of the kingdom of God has been given to you. But to those who do not know the secret, everything remains in parables so that, seeing they may see, and not perceive; and hearing they may hear, and not understand; lest haply they should turn again, and it should be forgiven them'.
>
> (Mark 4.10–12, Phillips).

The same is true today. Confronted by the unqualified certainties of Christ's revelation of the nature of God, men still divide themselves. I have tried to show in the previous two chapters that the main intention of Christ was to bring men to a true awareness of their own autistic predicament and, at the same time, to open them to the liberating knowledge that at the heart of reality lay utterly accepting Love. Our selfishness is an elaborate and tragic defence-mechanism against the threat which others pose to our radical insecurity; it is the consequence of some primordial anxiety which afflicts us, and which casts others and the universe itself in the role of Enemy. Christ came to cast out that fear by opening us to the knowledge that Reality was Love and that we need feel no insecurity as we face it. This was the redemption which he preached—freedom from the anxious bondage of the frightened ego. He taught men to address Reality as Father and to feel, in the universe, the freedom of sons in their father's house. Of course he did not offer men the shallow security of an easy time in this life. Indeed, in this life, he offered them a career of danger and turbulence.

> . . . beware of men: for they will deliver you up to the councils, and they will scourge you in their synagogues; and ye shall be brought before governors and kings for my sake . . . and ye shall be hated of all men for my name's sake: but he that endureth to the end shall be saved. (Matt. 10.17 ff.)

But to offer men worldly security, anyway, is always beside the point. Men feel an *ultimate* insecurity in the face of existence—that is the fundamental fact about man. It is true that they will translate this fundamental anxiety into many forms, and they will seek to assuage it in many ways, but the end result is always the same. His anxiety may drive a man to gain the whole world, but it will profit him nothing, since his anxiety is never quietened by the abundance of things which he possesses. Christ did not promise a life in which cancer would lose its power to kill or fire its power to consume; nor did he leave the world noticeably easier to endure. He was not the first Christian Scientist. What he offered was an ultimate security which enabled men to live with a joyful freedom which transcended tragedy in the midst of tragedy. Given this fundamental security, men could face the difficulties of existence with poise and trust. But this is no syllogism either, and it will make little sense to those who try to interpret it as such. The moment of release and recognition comes, or it doesn't, and I cannot tell why it comes to one and not to another, though I am certain that most men have had their moments of mysterious and heart-warming confidence in the meaning of life, whether or not they ask whence they came.

But so far we have been on reasonably negotiable ground. It is, after all, possible to paraphrase Christ's teaching about God into acceptably impersonal platitudes about 'confidence in life's meaning' or 'openness to the ground of our being'. There are many who will accept Christ's teaching in vaguely general terms like this, give or take a parable or two. But this is to avoid the main offence of the Christian faith. The first Christians were persuaded that Christ was more important for what he was than for what he said, which is the complete converse of the modern view. The earliest Christians spent years preaching Christ before they bothered to put his words down on paper to let us pick and choose. And here, I think, we have a clue to that mysterious rejection of Christ's teaching by many of his hearers which I have already noted. The fact seems to be that Christ's hearers felt that he was inseparable from his teaching. If he had merely set forth his opinions and insights about God in the abstract they would, doubtless, have argued or agreed. They were reasonable men, and reasonable men are always able to make a distinction between a man and his opinions, however unacceptable. Few of us agree with our friends on all important topics, but we rarely take up stones to cast at them. What was so different about Christ?

The fact seems to be that Christ's teaching about God was inseparably bound up with his own person. He not only taught men that God was accepting and forgiving love, he himself acted out or bodied-forth the nature of God by what he did. He not only taught men that God forgives to the uttermost; he himself forgave the sins of others. And not as you or I might forgive an offence committed against ourselves. *He forgave sins which had nothing, apparently, to do with him at all!* And who can forgive in this way, as the Jews justifiably remarked, save God? He not only taught that God was not bound and constrained by man's laws, which was one thing; he himself operated with complete disregard of them, which was quite another. And the way he taught had this same, disquieting characteristic. He did not, we are told, teach like the scribes who taught like good lawyers interpreting a law they could not alter; he taught with all the assurance and authority of one who *makes* law. He spoke, in short, as if he were God! And this is the precise nature of his offence. He was condemned for blasphemy as a man who behaved and talked as only God ought to: 'The Jews answered Pilate: we have a law, and by our law he ought to die, because he made himself [out to be] the Son of God.' (John 19.7.) The testimony of the first believers supports the accusation. Like their fellow-countrymen, they felt the inextricable conjunction between his teaching and his person. He revealed God by what he was and did, as well as by what he said. They were impelled not only to follow him as a wandering teacher, but to worship him as Lord. In him they had seen and kept company with 'the love that moves the sun and the other stars'.[1] This understanding of the nature of Christ is stated with defiant clarity in the First Letter of John:

> . . . it was *life* which appeared before us: we saw it, we are eyewitnesses of it, and are now writing to you about it. It was the very life of all ages, the life that has always existed with God the Father, which actually became visible in person to us mortal men. (1 John 1.2, Phillips)

Because the first Christians were personally convinced of the double nature of Christ long before they sought to interpret or explain the mystery of his person, they were certain from the beginning that his life was of more than *exemplary* significance. He was much more than the greatest in a long line of prophetic heroes who have heartened us by their example. Christ had a *representative* function which was unique. What happened to and through him had a universal significance and impact. The only way I can approach even the fringes of the cosmic significance of Christ is by means of the ancient doctrine of Substitution. When the first Christians claimed that Christ died for all men, they did not mean that he died *instead* of them. There are many better examples of this type of substitution: the man who throws himself upon an exploding hand-grenade is dying *instead of* his fellows. In that sense he is substituting his life for theirs. The priest who takes the place of the Jewish father bound for the Nazi death-camp is also a substitution in this sense.

These heroic acts of substitution have a real continuity with Christ's death, but there was a dimension to his sacrifice which was lacking in theirs. And here the full scandal of the Christian Gospel is laid bare, for the tradition dares, with an almost perplexed daring, to proclaim that in Christ God himself was suffering, for Christ was the *divine* Substitution. Theologians have been notoriously reluctant to approach the full scandal of this fact, and they have resorted to various semantic devices in order to protect their static conception of the immutability of God. This has given rise to a whole series of dubiously moral interpretations of the work of Christ, all of them involving a radical separation of the Son from the Father. The Father is conceived as sending forth his

Son to do the 'dirty work', while he remains safe and unchanging in the heavens.

Logic, of course, is the old enemy here. If religion is a syllogism, then our proclamation must somehow contrive to protect the passionless integrity of the Father. But if religion is a poem, then we can throw caution and logic to the winds and accept the full and flaring paradox of the Gospel: that in Christ God himself *suffered* and took unto himself the anguish and torment of Creation; that in Christ God *substituted himself* and endured the cross, despising the shame. And the very lunacy of the proclamation is its strongest claim. There is a sense in which the agony of the creation must be laid upon God as his responsibility. Any explanation which leaves Him out of the reckoning, protected by a sterile theo-logic, is profoundly unsatisfactory to the human heart, however appealing it may be to the arid intellect. There is a very real sense in which God's suffering children do rightly blame him, and with all the justice of the human heart call out to him to vindicate himself in the face of the monstrous tragedies of existence. Any explanation which suggests that man is only getting his just deserts for misusing his freedom, and that God stands apart, like a vindictive parent whose children have disobeyed his instructions, is monstrous. Man at his best is infinitely better than our theological aridities will allow God to be.

To vindicate himself in the eyes of the mother whose child has died in a napalm raid, God *must* suffer with her. He cannot remain aloof. It behoves God to go to the cross. The cross is the only sufficient vindication of God, and if the cross implies that God, somehow, is as powerless in the face of evil as we are, then let us face the hazardous implication without scuttling back into some semantic refuge which seeks to protect the omnipotence of God with a form of words. The only power of God which matters is the power of love and that, Christ proclaims, is the only and sufficient thing we need to know about God. *He loves and therefore he suffers*, and in the cross he advertises the fact that he trudges with us to all our calvaries, and will do so until the end of time. By this sublime act of substitution, Christ shows us that not only is God waiting for us at the end of all our striving as welcoming, accepting love; but that he is God in the midst of life, at this very moment bearing the burdens of his estranged Creation, like the parent of an autistic child who must, with endless and crucifying patience, bear the terrible effects of his son's condition in order to bring him to wholeness and normality. So the cross must not be seen as a brief and tragic episode, a mere event in time. It is a sublime and enduring fact, endlessly proclaiming the suffering of an endless love.

I want, now, to draw out some of the implications and aspects of this doctrine of Substitution by the interpretative technique I have used in previous chapters in an examination of another part of the New Testament narrative. I have called the crucifixion of Christ an 'action-parable', because it unfolds the nature and activity of God by means not of a teaching device, but of a substitutionary event. The representative character on the human side whom I shall seek to interpret is the Roman Governor who condemned Christ to death, Pontius Pilate. Our Lord's relationship with Pilate opens up to us the whole strategy of divine love.

> Then Pilate therefore took Jesus, and scourged him. And the soldiers platted a crown of thorns, and put it on his head, and they put on him a purple robe, and said, Hail, King of the Jews!

and they smote him with their hands. Pilate therefore went forth again, and saith unto them, Behold, I bring him forth to you, that ye may know that I find no fault in him. Then came Jesus forth, wearing the crown of thorns, and the purple robe. And Pilate saith unto them, Behold the man! When the chief priests therefore and officers saw him, they cried out, saying, Crucify him, crucify him. Pilate saith unto them, Take ye him, and crucify him: for I find no fault in him. The Jews answered him, We have a law, and by our law he ought to die, because he made himself the Son of God. When Pilate therefore heard that saying, he was the more afraid; and went again into the judgment hall, and saith unto Jesus, Whence art thou? But Jesus gave him no answer. Then saith Pilate unto him, Speakest thou not unto me? knowest thou not that I have power to crucify thee, and have power to release thee? Jesus answered, Thou couldest have no power at all against me, except it were given thee from above: therefore he that delivered me unto thee hath the greater sin. And from thenceforth Pilate sought to release him: but the Jews cried out, saying, If thou let this man go, thou art not Caesar's friend: whosoever maketh himself a king speaketh against Caesar. When Pilate therefore heard that saying, he brought Jesus forth, and sat down in the judgment seat in a place that is called the Pavement, but in the Hebrew, Gabbatha. And he saith unto the Jews, Behold your King! But they cried out, Away with him, away with him, crucify him. Pilate saith unto them, Shall I crucify your King? The chief priests answered, We have no king but Caesar. Then delivered he him therefore unto them to be crucified. And they took Jesus, and led him away. And he bearing his cross went forth unto a place called the place of a skull, . . . where they crucified him . . . (John 19.1–18.)

Dorothy L. Sayers, in *The Man Born to be King*, describes a dream which came to Claudia Procla, the wife of Pontius Pilate.

PILATE: Claudia, Claudia, tell me—what was this dream of yours?

CLAUDIA: I was in a ship at sea, voyaging among the islands of the Aegean. At first the weather seemed calm and sunny—but presently, the sky darkened—and the sea began to toss with the wind . . . Then out of the east, there came a cry, strange and piercing . . . 'Pan ho megas tethnéke——Pan ho megas tethnéke—— . . . and I said to the captain, 'What do they cry?' And he answered, 'Great Pan is dead'. And I asked him, 'How can God die?' And he answered, 'Don't you remember? They crucified him. He suffered under Pontius Pilate.' . . . Then all the people in the ship turned their faces to me and said: 'Pontius Pilate . . . Pontius Pilate . . . he suffered under Pontius Pilate . . . crucified, dead and buried . . . sub Pontio Pilato . . . Pilato . . . he suffered . . . suffered . . . under Pontius Pilate . . . under Pontius Pilate . . .' . . . in all tongues and all voices . . . even the little children with their mothers '. . . Suffered under Pontius Pilate . . . sub Pontio Pilato . . . crucifié sous Ponce Pilate . . . gekreuzigt unter Pontius Pilatus' . . . your name, husband, your name continually—'he suffered under Pontius Pilate'.[2]

Claudia Procla heard her husband's name sounding through the centuries, and so, of course, it has. The Christian creeds have carried the message down the ages: 'Jesus Christ, his only Son, our Lord, . . . suffered under Pontius Pilate, was crucified, dead and buried'. 'One Lord, Jesus Christ was crucified also for us under Pontius Pilate. He suffered and and was buried . . .' Pontius Pilate. Why has the Church put his name in her Creed?

The obvious answer, though not the most important one, is that the use of this name firmly fixes the crucifixion of Jesus Christ in history. We are dealing here with an event as definite as today's headlines. He was crucified 'under Pontius Pilate'. Pilate was governor of Judea from A.D. 26 to 36, when he was recalled to Rome. We know a fair bit about him. He showed very little understanding of the Jews whom he was sent to govern, though, to be fair, few Romans would have known how to deal with a people as possessed by their religion as were the Jews. Early on in his term of office he caused a violent disturbance by using Temple funds to build an aqueduct; and there is evidence that on two or three occasions he was ruthless in suppressing religious violence. But one can sympathise with him. Religious bitterness is very difficult to deal with. The nearest modern parallel I can think of—and, of course, it is far from exact—is the situation in Northern Ireland today. Imagine a tough yet fastidiously agnostic career diplomat sent to govern Northern Ireland by force, a situation seething with religious and political tension. Can you imagine his frustration, disdain and final cynicism as he picks his way through confrontation after confrontation with the invincible irrationality of opposed extremists? No: Pontius Pilate had a difficult job to do, and it is to his credit that he stuck it for ten years.

Towards the end of his stay in Judea he gave permission for the execution of Jesus of Nazareth. It happened about the year 33. Pontius Pilate and his wife were both impressed by Jesus and, according to Matthew, he did try to release him at her request. But by this time he was a cynical and probably exhausted man. So, with a disdainful gesture, he washed his hands of the whole affair, and handed over Jesus to be crucified. In the year 33 Jesus Christ was crucified under Pontius Pilate, he suffered and was buried.

We don't know what happened to Pilate after that. He steps out of history, though legends abound. One has it that he later became a Christian, and the Abyssinian Church has canonised him. Another legend has it that, like Judas Iscariot, he later committed suicide. There are legends, too, about his wife, Claudia Procla. The Greek Church canonised her. We cannot, of course, be certain of any of these things. All we know for certain is that during his term of office as Governor of Judea he crucified Jesus, and his name passed into history for that reason only. The name Pontius Pilate has been a date-stamp on the Christian creed ever since.

But there is another reason why Pontius Pilate is in the creed, and this reason is more important and more complex. To understand it, we must open ourselves to the bewildering complexity of human history. This is difficult for us, for most of us have been brought up on 'the good guys versus the bad guys' theory of history. In fact, history and human nature are much more complicated than that. I want to illustrate this by citing an example from fairly recent history. The paradigm of the complexity I wish to explore is provided by Winston Churchill. A few years ago I saw the controversial play by the German playwright, Hochhuth, called *The Soldiers*. In this play, Hochhuth tried to prove that Churchill was a war criminal. But apart altogether from that sensational accusation (which was forcefully and convincingly repudiated), the play raises a fascinating and insoluble human dilemma. Churchill went to war to defeat the monstrous evil of Nazi Germany. It was Germany's invasion of Poland that brought Britain into the war. Towards the end of the conflict, in the play, things are still in the balance and Churchill is in an appalling dilemma. He cannot defeat Germany without Russia's help, yet Stalin's Russia is as great an evil as Hitler's Germany. In order to make certain that Russia will not make an independent arrangement with Germany and turn against the Allies, Churchill has to turn a blind eye to Russia's occupation of the eastern European countries, including Poland. It is expedient that Poland be sacrificed to Russia, rather than have the whole of Europe perish beneath a double tyranny. Poland brought Britain into the war, but in order to win the war Poland must be sacrificed. And here we see the hideous anguish of the man of power. What Churchill did, according to Hochhuth, was evil, but it was unavoidable. He sacrificed Poland and Czechoslovakia and all those eastern European countries which are still Russian satellites, in order to save the rest of Europe from another Hitler–Stalin pact.

What would we have done in his place? Here we face an appalling human dilemma. The affairs of men rarely allow for a simple choice between an obvious good and an obvious evil, between light and darkness. Very often, whatever we choose to do is wrong, because there is something profoundly wrong with human nature and it vitiates all our choices. There is a profound distortion at the root of things which makes all our choices corrupt to some degree. This tragic and indelible flaw in man's nature vitiates even his noblest actions. And this was Pilate's dilemma. He was in an appalling situation. If he released Jesus he would provoke a riot, many would be killed, and reports would be sent to Rome. His own continuing usefulness in a tense situation would be compromised. On the other hand, Jesus is innocent of any charge which merits the death-sentence, and Pilate knows it; and the whole genius of Roman law was, in theory, for the protection of the rights of man. How was he to act? Jesus recognised his dilemma and had compassion upon him, compassion because he was in a position of power. 'Thou couldest have no power at all against me, except it were given thee from above: therefore he that delivered me unto thee hath the greater sin'. By these words of Christ to Pilate the Christian is called upon to feel compassion for those trapped in the dilemmas of human power, to pray for them and to sympathise with them in their difficulties.

Pilate, of course, made the inevitable decision; the only decision he could possibly make in the circumstances: he sacrificed one innocent man for the sake of maintaining peace. It was expedient. Churchill and Poland. Pilate and Christ. What other decision was humanly possible? We would have done the same. And yet we know both decisions were evil—evil, yet unavoidable; evil, yet inevitable. What is this tragic flaw in humanity that forces us to these decisions? For they are *our* decisions. Churchill and Pilate are our representatives. They are Everyman. And we have acted like them, time after time. We have turned our backs on the needs of others, on the demands they make on us, because we have other responsibilities, other considerations which must be taken into account. We have families, we have jobs, we have unavoidable obligations. And we do have these obligations and we cannot run away from them. We live in the midst of excruciating dilemmas. Liberation only comes when I recognise that I, and not another, am Pontius Pilate. Every day I make the unavoidable decision to hand over Christ. He suffered under Pontius Pilate; was crucified, dead and buried. *I* am Pontius Pilate and he allows himself to suffer at my hands. These are the most momentous and comforting words in history. In Christ, God the Substitute loves us and pities our dilemmas. He has compassion upon our impossible predicament. He stretches out towards us just as we are, soiled with compromises, heavy with the burden of evil decisions, laden with greater and lesser infidelities. I am Pontius Pilate, and he allows himself to suffer under my hand. He does not hold back till I make the right decisions, till I purify myself. He comes to me recognising my unavoidable sinfulness, and accepts me in spite of it. And the cross is the demonstration of this incredible love, the suffering love of the divine Substitute who bears the consequence of my fear and regret and anxiety. He does not judge us and condemn us in our dilemmas; he himself becomes the victim of our dilemmas. He takes them and bears them in his own body on the tree.

So Pontius Pilate is in the creed because he is my representative. By this name we celebrate the heart-wrenching truth that God allows himself to suffer at our hands. This is how he deals with my sin: he takes the consequences of it upon himself. He knows my dilemmas and weaknesses and he takes them upon himself. And as I lay the cross upon his back, day after day, he gazes at me with compassion. The crucifixion of Christ is the most luminous event in history, and its significance resounds throughout all time. The execution of Christ is not just another statistic in that endless roll of human suffering. It is that certainly, but it is more, much more than that. The Christian tradition has sung the significance of this event with all the passion of impossibility. It has declaimed the mysterious poetry of a man nailed to those rough beams who was very God of very God; God himself, powerless on a cross; the Creator of all things, victim and slave. It means that at the heart of all reality, woven through the fabric of a tragic universe, there is a suffering God who shares Calvary with his creation. It means that our God is no distant spectator of his creation's anguish; he is himself victim of the torment. In the cross God gives us the answer to the cruel riddle of evil and suffering in a way that is deeper than words. He gives us a poem not a syllogism. He shows us that he is in the midst of the conflict. We have Christ's own words for it: he is imprisoned with us, he hungers and thirsts with us, he is the child and the mother to whom it clings in that death-camp out there beyond sanity. He is within the tomb and beside the grave. God himself is in the midst of us, trudging with us to all our calvaries. He is in anguish until the end of time.

And that, and that alone is our great and unconquerable hope, because it means that the cross is not just an isolated event in history; it is as old as God's love; it is an eternal fact. It is a sign to us that God himself is engaged in a costly battle with the mystery of evil which haunts his creation. Though the outcome is not in doubt, the struggle is terrible and wounds the very hands of God. And while the sky grows dark and the Jordan swells he sets this emblem of the cross above the battle to comfort and sustain us with the knowledge that he is at our side, even in the darkest valley. This emblem of the costly love of God has comforted and sustained men for centuries. They have written songs about it. They have painted and carved it. And they have clutched it to them as they entered the shadow of death. The cross, the faithful cross, 'one and only, noble tree'.

But the poem of divine Substitution did not end on Good Friday. If it had, none of these pages would have been written, nor millions besides. Christ's life and death would be remembered, if remembered at all, as simply another wistful tragedy of a good man crushed by a bullying universe. This was clearly the first verdict of his earliest followers as they dispersed on that bleak Friday. The song of the Cross, which celebrated the sweetest wood and sweetest iron of that gaunt instrument of torture, was composed retrospectively, as was the whole New Testament. Any book about the Christian Faith ought, therefore, to start at the Resurrection, since everything we know about Christ from the Tradition was written from the perspective of the knowledge of his rising again. What we know about Christ is already illuminated by and interpreted through his Resurrection. We know no other Christ than the Risen Christ, for no other type of record exists. We either know Christ risen or we do not know him at all. This book, then, will end at the beginning.

10

The Restoration

THE EVALUATION and interpretation of the Resurrection narratives in the New Testament has become one of the major theological growth industries of our era. According to New Testament scholars (and I see no reason to disagree with them) the Resurrection narratives are a complex tangle of genuine recollection and later interpretation. Significantly, Joachim Jeremias subtitles his chapter on the Easter story in the first volume of his *New Testament Theology*, 'The earliest tradition and the earliest interpretation'. He maintains convincingly that the record as we have it is a mixture of both basic tradition and interpretative elaboration upon the tradition, usually with an apologetic motive. 'If genuine recollection is reflected in the variety of people and locations mentioned in the accounts, other features can be recognised as secondary elaborations.'[1]

New Testament scholars are engaged in a permanent debate as to what is 'genuine' and what is 'secondary'. Since the debate is carried on at a lofty level, involving minute knowledge of the arcane science of textual criticism and an easy familiarity with several dead languages and their surviving literature, it is not easy for the layman to come to any personal conclusions on the matter. He must, perforce, accept on trust the conclusions of his chosen guides. But the matter is complicated further by the fact that the guides do not agree among themselves. When, for instance, Rudolf Bultmann and Joachim Jeremias, two men of enormous erudition, who have spent their whole lives on the subject and have both written thousands of words about it, disagree radically both in their approach and in the conclusions they reach, how am I, with only a smattering of Greek and a novice's knowledge of textual criticism, to make up my mind? Intuitively, I find Jeremias more to my taste, but many of my brethren are equally devout in their allegiance to Bultmann. I suspect that here, as in many other places, a man's glands have as much to do with his approach to the subject as anything else, though he will rarely thank you for pointing this out. In this, as in most things,

> Every boy and every gal
> That's born into the world alive
> Is either a little liberal
> Or else a little conservative.[2]

If this were all that could be said about it we'd be in an intolerable predicament. Fortunately, this is not where the real offence lies. The dispute about the textual reliability or otherwise of the New Testament narratives is both secondary and technical, since the fundamental problem lies not with the texts but with the event which occasioned them. There will be no end in this life to the textual dispute. It will continue to provide a fruitful and fascinating topic for investigation and disagreement for centuries. The fascination of the task is not restrained but deepened by its fundamental insolubility.

Like the identity of the Dark Lady in Shakespeare's sonnets, it will continue to provide an occupation for scholarly minds until the Day of Judgement brings other preoccupations. We can safely lay the dispute on one side and fall to the real matter at hand, very much in the way that we can enjoy Shakespeare while knowing nothing of the Dark Lady or the scholarly uproar that surrounds her.

The reason for this is simple: the whole New Testament presupposes and is activated by a belief in the Resurrection. The 'genuine' elements in the text as well as their alleged 'secondary' elaborations are all premised upon the basic claim that the Resurrection *happened*. Since it is the Resurrection itself which is the real issue, no interrogation of the texts as texts will help us to resolve our attitude to that primal mystery: the texts take it for granted; they do not argue about it. No matter how sharply you pare away the alleged secondary accretions, you are still left with the simple fact that when we first find the early Church it is already preaching the Resurrection of Christ, *and all our records date from that period.* The New Testament is already a witness to the Resurrection when we take it up, and our problem is deepened for us because we cannot get back to any other independent account of these events. The New Testament is the only witness we have, and it is a witness with its mind already made up and long past changing. The only thing we can do, therefore, is to examine the claims it makes, decide how reliable a witness it is, and come to our own conclusions.

According to Jeremias, the earliest written account demonstrates just how difficult it is to get an overall view of the sequence of events in question. In 1 Corinthians 15. 3–8, Paul tells us:

> I taught you what I had been taught myself, namely that Christ died for our sins, in accordance with scriptures; that he was buried; and that he was raised to life on the third day, in accordance with the scriptures; that he appeared first to Cephas and secondly to the Twelve. Next he appeared to more than five hundred of the brothers at the same time, most of whom are still alive, though some have died; then he appeared to James, and then to all the apostles; and last of all he appeared to me too; it was as though I was born when no one expected it.

Jeremias reminds us that this passage, which is the earliest account we have of the Resurrection, is not a complete list of the post-Resurrection Christophanies, although that is possibly what Paul set out to provide. In an important footnote Jeremias makes this comment:

> The absence of Mary of Magdala (John 20.14–18) or the two Maries (Matt. 28.1, 9f) from the six-membered list in 1 Cor. 15.5–8 could be explained by the fact that the testimony of women was not acceptable; it might be just possible to explain the absence of Joseph and Matthias (Acts 1.22f) by including them among the five hundred brethren (1 Cor. 15.6), but that would still leave the disciples on the road to Emmaus (Luke 24.13–35), the seven on Lake Gennesaret (John 21.1–14) and Stephen (Acts 7.56) unaccounted for.[3]

In spite of the difficulties illustrated by this passage, it is still possible to isolate, if not the exact sequence of events, then the central claim which is being made. In Paul the main impact lies in the careful use of the passive verb 'egēgertai': 'he was raised up'. There are three connected elements in this central claim of the New Testament.

1. Christ truly died and was buried. The finality of this death is emphasised in different ways by all the New Testament writers.

2. He was *raised* from the dead. It is never suggested that Christ's Resurrection was simply a form of psychic survival or the release of his spirit from the prison of the body. Paul's use of the passive is as emphatic in its way as is the emphasis upon the empty tomb in the Gospels: Christ's Resurrection was not a resurrection *from* the body but *with* the body. It was not the survival or immortality of Christ's spirit which the Church preached (a claim which would have occasioned little offence at the time); it was quite clearly the Resurrection of the whole Christ, including his body. I am not, at this stage, making any evaluation of the claim. I simply wish to set forth what the claim is. The New Testament clearly understands that Christ's corpse was raised from the tomb by an act of divine power. This fact is clearly underlined by the tradition of the empty tomb and the accusation which was flung at the young community that the disciples had stolen the body.

> The chief priests held a meeting with the elders and, after some discussion, handed a considerable sum of money to the soldiers with these instructions, 'This is what you must say, "His disciples came during the night and stole him away while we were asleep". And should the governor come to hear of this, we undertake to put things right with him ourselves and to see that you do not get into trouble.' The soldiers took the money and carried out their instructions, and to this day that is the story among the Jews. (Matt. 28.12–15.)

It was this claim about the body of Christ which exposed the Christian community to doubt and ridicule.

> A few Epicurean and Stoic philosophers argued with Paul. Some said, 'Does this parrot know what he's talking about?' And, because he was preaching about Jesus and the resurrection, others said, 'He sounds like a propagandist for some outlandish gods'. (Acts 17.18.)

An interpretation of the Resurrection as a purely spiritualistic survival would not have exposed them to this type of reaction, yet the records go out of their way to make their claim quite explicit. Jeremias says that certain secondary elements in the text have an apologetic motive which is clearly aimed at affirming the corporeality of the Risen Christ, sometimes to the point of coarseness.

> They were still talking about all this when he himself stood among them and said to them, 'Peace be with you!' In a state of alarm and fright, they thought they were seeing a ghost. But he said, 'Why are you so agitated, and why are these doubts rising in your hearts? Look at my hands and feet; yes, it is I indeed, Touch me and see for yourselves; a ghost has no flesh and bones as you can see I have'. And as he said this he showed them his hands and feet. Their joy was so great that they still could not believe it, and they stood there dumbfounded; so he said to them, 'Have you anything to eat?' And they offered him a piece of grilled fish, which he took and ate before their eyes. (Luke 24.36–43.)

He overcomes final doubts by eating grilled fish before the disciples' eyes, and in a variant to this same passage the disciples give the Lord a piece of honeycomb as well as the fish, 'the remainder of which the Risen Lord then hands back; the purpose of this is evidently that the disciples shall have a tangible piece of evidence in the form of the impression of his teeth in the honeycomb.'[4] I am not, let me repeat, interested at this point in assessing the credibility or otherwise of this evidence; rather, since the only evidence we have comes from the Church, it is important to discover what they actually believed had taken place, since that is as close as we can get to the events themselves. It is notoriously easy to read one's own preconceptions into these early records. I am trying, as far as I can, to hold this impulse back for a moment and simple allow the conviction of the early Christian community to confront us. It is quite clear that, at the point in time represented by the New Testament accounts, the mind of the Church is convinced that Christ's resurrection body is in direct continuity with his corporeal body, while, at the same time, it inhabits a whole new dimension of being which is free of the limitations of purely corporeal existence.

3. He *appeared* to his followers after his Resurrection. Hering's note on 1 Corinthians 15.5 is interesting for the emphasis it lays upon Paul's conviction about the objectivity of the Resurrection: 'Paul gives proofs of the historicity of the resurrection, not by the empty tomb, of which he never speaks, but by the appearances.'[5] It was these totally unexpected Christophanies which finally emboldened the earliest followers to shake off the misery which had shrouded them since Good Friday. Henceforth their lives were totally reoriented round this pivotal experience, and Christ's life and significance would be preached and interpreted in the light of his Resurrection. It would be impossible to return to a pre-resurrection objectivity in their account of Christ. 'Even if we did once know Christ in the flesh, that is not how we know him now' (2 Cor. 5.16). From now on their very memories of Christ in the flesh would be bathed in the afterglow of Easter. Many scholars believe that certain recorded events in our Lord's life, such as his Transfiguration, are post-resurrection appearances read back into the record of his earthly life. In the same way, many believe that Christ's predictions of his Resurrection belong to the same retrospective law, especially since his followers seemed totally demoralised by his death and completely unprepared for his

rising again. This whole penumbra of doubt and confusion is captured by Jeremias in a fascinating passage:

> . . . The characteristic feature of the *earliest stratum of tradition* is that it still preserves a recollection of the overpowering, puzzling and mysterious nature of the events: eyes opened at the breaking of the bread, beams of heavenly light, a figure on the shore at break of day, the unexpected appearance in a closed room, the outbreak of praise expressed in speaking with tongues, the sudden disappearance—all these are ways in which the earliest tradition is formulated. The same mysterious *chiaroscuro* surrounds the earliest accounts of the reactions of the witnesses: now they fail to recognise the Risen One, now the heavenly brightness blinds them, now they believe that they have seen a ghost. Fear and trembling, anxiety, uncertainty and doubt struggle with joy and worship. 'None of the disciples dared ask him, "Who are you?" They knew it was the Lord' (John 21.12). 'When they saw him they worshipped him; but some doubted' (Matt. 28.17). There is no hesitation in confessing, 'They (simply) could not believe (it) for joy' (Lk. 24.41).[6]

The simple and obvious fact is that the early followers of our Lord experienced the Resurrection as a massive and climactic crisis which altered their total orientation towards the past as well as towards the present and the future. It was a turning-point which left nothing unaltered, and it can only be likened to one of those evolutionary transitions or jumps which result in vast qualitative and quantitative changes in the history of the earth, the major difference being that this vast evolutionary leap was experienced in days rather than millennia. This, anyway, is how it seemed to them. The nature of the crisis is best measured in its impact on individuals. In the case of Peter and Paul, for instance, this event split their lives in two. Paul says of his experience of the risen Christ that it resulted in an entirely new life: 'the old creation has gone, and now the new one is here.' And certainly for Paul, his encounter with the risen Christ produced a massive moral and psychological crisis which changed the direction and quality of his whole life. The same was true for Peter and for the whole group he led, which was dramatically changed from a dispirited bunch of deserters into a force which changed the whole direction of history. And these are *facts*, however we interpret them. It is a fact that the early Church, when we first discover it in history, is making these extraordinary claims. And it is also a fact that, however *we* interpret the claim they make, it profoundly altered their lives and through them the lives of millions of others.

What are we to make of the event which initiated these far-reaching effects? And it is important to underline the fact that we only know the event through its effects. There is no description in the New Testament of the Resurrection itself, only a record of the effects it produced. We have the inside claims of the early community, and they concern happenings which are no longer examinable by us. First of all, there is the disappearance of the dead body of Christ. This is the most difficult part of the evidence for a twentieth-century Western man to accept, formed and governed as he is by the unconscious agenda of the objective consciousness. It does not persuade him, either, to point out that the resurrection of a dead body was just as unprecedented and conceptually impossible for a first-century Jew as for twentieth-century Europeans.

> There is nothing comparable to the resurrection of Jesus anywhere in Jewish literature. Certainly there are mentions of raisings from the dead, but these are always resuscitations, a return to earthly life. Nowhere in Jewish literature do we have a resurrection to glory as an event of history.[7]

No, the whole thing was just as difficult to accept 2000 years ago as it is today. The irreversible finality of death was just as much a fact then as it is now, and only that innate intellectual fascism in our attitude to the past which is such a mark of our era can persuade us otherwise. The first proclamation of the Resurrection was met with ridicule and incredulity, even within the earliest group of our Lord's followers. How are we to account for this claim? If the opponents of our Lord had stolen the body, its production would have scotched the claims of his followers finally and effectively. This was never done. It is equally inconceivable that the whole thing was a hoax perpetrated by the disciples. First of all, because a hoax of this sort would inevitably have been uncovered by the determined opposition of the authorities. More importantly, because it is psychologically inconceivable that the disciples, who were broken and totally demoralised by the events of Good Friday, could have put together such an absurd fabrication, especially since to maintain such a deception would have called for a steely and determined courage, a characteristic which was conspicuously absent from our Lord's followers on the day of his death. And to what end would such a fraud have been perpetrated, since anything less likely to be believed could scarcely be imagined?

Even more convincingly, do men die heroes' deaths for a hoax they themselves have perpetrated? And is it conceivable that such a monstrous and transparent deceit could have won the co-operation and acceptance of the early Church's most brilliant and implacable opponent, Saul of Tarsus? And how are we to account for the initial disbelief and confusion of the disciples, so clearly and unflatteringly represented in the tradition? The most self-authenticating aspect of the whole story is precisely the fact that no one seemed prepared for what happened; everyone was taken by surprise. This surprise and perplexity runs through every strand of the narrative. On a purely evidential level, therefore, the disappearance of the body of Jesus is a fact which cannot be dismissed, simply because it does not conform to our preconceptions about stable and predictable reality. The whole Resurrection event is something that shatters all preconceptions and stubbornly refuses to fit into our tidy arrangements. While we cannot examine the central core of the event, we must make an honest attempt to evaluate its effects. And all the alternative explanations for the absence of the body of Christ seem to be intrinsically less convincing than the explanation given by the disciples.

At any rate, the earliest disciples were convinced that the body of Christ had gone. We must ask ourselves whether or not they are reliable witnesses, and if we find in the negative, then surely we must come up with a convincing alternative explanation. All the alternative explanations, it seems to me, imply the moral and intellectual inferiority of a group of men the splendour of whose subsequent behaviour utterly belies this initially monumental act of fraud or gullible *naïveté*. If we cannot accept their testimony on this crucial and foundational event, how can we believe anything they say? And I am not persuaded that in a matter like this, where the fundamental integrity of the first Christian community is at stake, we can afford to remain agnostic.

The discovery of the empty tomb and the subsequent failure of the disciples to find the body gave rise to an understandable fear and anxiety which was only relieved by the second 'effect' of the Resurrection event, the series of appearances of the risen Christ. Today, we can only validate the integrity of these appearances by their impact upon the disciples, and that impact, as I have already indicated, was immeasurable. It transformed a small and not terribly bright collection of puzzled artisans into a joyful and invincible army of believers. This is an incontestable fact of history, and it demands a verdict from us which will be consistent with the evidence which faces us.

It seems impossible to interpret the internal evidence for the Resurrection, evidence which, as I have already noted, is only provided by the Resurrection community itself, in any other way than they did. We cannot overturn the evidence convincingly from within. We cannot argue the facts they provide into any other verdict than the one they proclaimed. There is no other way of adding up the evidence as they provide it. But opponents of the Resurrection do not, in any case, do this. They never succeed in turning the evidence as such in any other direction. When the Resurrection is denied it is not denied on internal grounds based on a valid alternative interpretation of the given evidence, but on external *a priori* grounds, which hold that the whole thing is intrinsically impossible. It says that the Resurrection *did not* happen because it *could not* happen. Since it is inconceivable that Christ's body was raised, the disciples must have been mistaken about the facts. Christ's bones lie beneath some Galilean hillside because they cannot possibly be anywhere else, since bones cannot be raised from the dead. It is as simple as that. Mistaken about the empty tomb and the disappearance of Christ's body, the disciples were equally mistaken as to the objective content of the so-called appearances. They were probably a form of mass hysteria, triggered by 'foolish women' and the swollen and disappointed longing of the dead man's followers. So the Resurrection narratives and the subsequent history of the Church are really the story of an exceedingly powerful and creative illusion, and centuries of the Christian experience are simply the self-perpetuating effects of the greatest non-event in history.

At first sight, this version of events may appear to be incontestably rational, given what we know about the natural workings of the universe, but it contains several flaws and is not quite as self-authenticating as it may at first appear.

First of all, it begs the whole question in advance of an examination of the only evidence available, by refusing to admit even the theoretical possibility of a resurrection. To refuse to examine proof of a man's innocence because you have already decided in advance that he must be guilty, without reference to any evidence other than your own preconceived notions, is neither just nor rational. It is on that totalitarian level that the Christian claims for the factuality of the Resurrection are currently repudiated.

Secondly, it presents us with the enormous difficulty of finding extenuating reasons for convictions held so fiercely by a group of men and women whom we find admirable on other grounds. To resolve the problem of the Resurrection by a condescending refusal to discuss the matter because of its intrinsic impossibility only leaves you with the enormous moral problem of dealing with a band of men and women who are just as capable of recognising an impossibility when they see it as we are, and who yet insist that this very impossibility has occurred; and who stick to their insistence with a nonchalant heroism which does not waver even in the face of persecution and death. And let me repeat myself again.

The Resurrection was no less scandalous and impossible and totally without precedent or analogy for first-century man than for us. It was not easier for them to accept than it is for us, though we easily persuade ourselves that it was. The Resurrection was an offence from the very beginning; and the disciples knew this, and bore the brunt of the offence in their own bodies, and stuck to their account even unto death, because they were utterly persuaded that he was risen and was alive for evermore. It seems to me that only a very cynical and attenuated consciousness can dismiss this phenomenon with such theoretical detachment.

There are many others, however, who cannot believe in the Resurrection, yet who desperately want to. They are impressed and strangely haunted by the testimony of the first disciples, and they long for a similar certainty of settled conviction. But it doesn't happen. The moment of recognition never comes. He never meets them in the garden before daybreak and speaks the word that lifts the veil from their eyes. What of them? Here, of course, we have worked full circle, for the Resurrection of Jesus Christ, like the existence of God, can never be demonstrated on purely evidential grounds. It is a poem, not a syllogism. A man's mind may be theoretically persuaded by the arguments for the existence of God and the historicity of the Resurrection, and he may still remain an unbeliever, because belief is a deeply personal thing: it is a moment of meeting, a sudden surge of recognition, a rapture of man's whole being which catches him out of himself in an adoring awareness of the other. It happens or it doesn't, and we cannot command its happening. So, in an important sense, the historical factuality of the Resurrection is irrelevant unless and until it can become true for me.

But we must immediately affirm the other side of the paradox, which is that it cannot be true for me existentially unless it is first true absolutely. Neither God nor the Resurrection of Christ depend upon my awareness for their reality. It is not my faith which conjures them into existence. Nevertheless, the problem of Faith is always a personal problem, in which the unbeliever asks, 'How can this be true for me?' I dare to suggest that this question is already a question which is spoken from Faith, for the searcher is always one who, in Augustine's words, would not be searching if he had not, in some sense, already found. The longing is already an aspect of belief, for we cannot long for something of which we know nothing. The longing is already a recognition and an awareness. It may be that, in the kind of culture we have created, longing is a profoundly contemporary mode of Faith; the longing of those for whom the sun is eclipsed, though the darkness is shot through with joy and a strange expectancy. It seems to me that for a man in that condition, and it is frequently my own, the only possible line of action is to live as though the darkness were already light and the night as clear as the day. Since a man must choose, it is better to choose defiantly and to live according to one's deepest longings than to settle back into the grey world of trivial and unadventurous certainty. Our Lord told us there were some men who could only enter the Kingdom of Heaven by violence; they storm it with the longing of desperation. It is certainly better to do that than to do nothing. After all, no sane man stops work and goes to bed simply because the sun is in eclipse. He carries on as usual, waiting, waiting for the shadow to pass from the light.

One of the many advantages of an institutional or corporate

faith like Christianity is that it allows many gradations of commitment and belief to individuals, while retaining an essential standard of faith for the whole community. The standard is the corporate expression of that faith as it has been held and handed on down the centuries. The individual's personal apprehension of the faith may be meagre and hesitant, fraught with private doubt and the limitations of his own historical situation. Nevertheless, it is still possible for him to confess the total faith of the community because it is the *community's* and because he wishes to identify himself with the community, if only by intention. Christian Faith is essentially a communal faith. Inevitably, the faith of the universal community (and it is important to remember that that universality includes time as well as space, the past as well as the present) will be stronger and more clearly articulated than the private apprehensions of the individual Christian. One of the many advantages of this corporateness is that it allows the individual space for personal growth and doubt, while retaining a loyalty to the corporate standard *as* a corporate standard.

This is partly a matter of what we might call methodological humility, a working arrangement whereby we don't push our own subjective insights and difficulties too far. Only a silly and arrogant man will insist on elevating his own subjective apprehensions to the level of infallible certainty. A moment of self-examination will demonstrate the folly of this procedure. Both individuals and cultures are notoriously volatile in their attitudes. The certainties of one generation inevitably become the target for another generation's withering ridicule. This is certainly true of theological fashions. Let me give one example from fairly recent history.

The theology of Western Christianity between the two world wars is usually characterised as 'the social gospel'. It was optimistic about man; it laid great stress upon the immanence of God in his creation; it had a heavily ethical emphasis, and called men briskly to the work of building the Kingdom of heaven here on earth. But this rather liberal and humanistic version of Christianity was soon found to be a totally inappropriate response to the massive evils of totalitarian politics. It took the twin trumpet-blasts of Reinhold Niebuhr and Karl Barth to recall theologians to a rediscovery of the misery and sinfulness of man and of that majesty and transcendence of God which alone could stand against his destructive pride. Since those days, theological fashions have shuddered from atheism to ecstasy and back again with hectic irregularity. The *corporate* nature of faith, therefore, is our greatest safeguard against the vagaries of our own subjectivism and the hysteria of fashionable witch-doctors. The paradox of such a corporate standard is that it allows a greater scope to genuine doubt than would be the case if the Faith were brought out in new editions every generation. The unbeliever, who longs to believe but cannot, is able to enter the community of Faith as an act of experimental defiance. He is like the mystic in the dark night of the soul who clings to the objectivity of the liturgy, though his prayer is arid and without consolation. It is the *objectivity* of the Faith which is his safeguard. He can will the Faith long before and long after he has ceased to feel it. But when you reduce the Faith to what an individual or a culture can personally accept or apprehend at any given time, you replace faith with subjectivity, and man becomes his own standard. And this is the very tragedy from which Faith sought to liberate man in the first place. It is man's tragedy that he is constantly impelled to set himself up as the norm and standard of all value. This is his radical egoism, and like all egoism it is self-defeating. He can only be released from his autistic predicament when he is enabled to will Another as the norm and standard of all significance. And how is he to do this if his own subjectivity is the test of Faith? This is perhaps the cruellest trick which a minimalist theology plays upon man, since it offers him no escape from the bondage of his own subjectivity.

Of course, there are dangers in this corporate understanding of faith. There is the danger of the zealot who insists on applying every aspect of the historic tradition as a test of the integrity of the believer. These tests have brought the objectivity of the Faith into disrepute by encouraging hypocrisy and dishonesty. The zealot and the reductionist (who errs in the opposite direction by making his private insight the test of integrity) both share a fundamental misconception about the nature of Faith. They are both rigorists who insist, in their different ways, on an exact correspondence between the Faith and the believer, thereby making the human response of primary importance. In fact, the Faith is simply an articulation of the love of God which is there before our apprehension of it, and is the very ground and motive of our own responding love. There can never be an exact correspondence or even an approximate correspondence between God's love and man's response, or between the Faith and the believer's apprehension of it. It is the glorious objectivity of God's love, *apart altogether from man's response*, which is our liberation. It is there, even when we do not and cannot believe it with our whole heart or mind, and the

Faith is simply the historic articulation of that releasing certainty. This is why, at the end of the day, the task of the Church is proclamation rather than persuasion. We do not exist to persuade people to accept a series of unverifiable propositions. On the contrary, by some mysterious humour of the Divine Will we have been called to the menial task of acting as witnesses to an event we do not entirely understand. We are not even given the arduous dignity of the task of advocacy. 'There is an Advocate for the Father', the Holy Spirit of God, whose work of pleading the Divine Mercy is an endless pressure on man's heart. Our task is much simpler: it is to maintain the task of corporate witness to the Resurrection. It is the Holy Spirit who convinces men of the reliability of our outrageous testimony. We simply proclaim the vision we have received as a community and struggle to apprehend as individuals.

What, then, is the vision which has been handed down through the testimony of the Universal Church? What does the Resurrection mean? Of all the New Testament writers, Paul is the most fruitful source of metaphors and analogies which open up something of the meaning of the great Resurrection vision. He takes his metaphors from the world of law or commerce or agriculture, telling us that the Resurrection of Christ is a pledge or first instalment of a glorious future which is in store for the whole creation; or that it is the first sheaf in God's great task of bringing his whole creation to a triumphant harvest of joy and hope. Emboldened by his daring use of analogy, let me attempt a more modern illustration for interpreting the significance of this great event.

The best modern analogy I can think of is taken from the

cinema. The Resurrection of Jesus Christ is like a film-preview advertising, as they put it, 'a future presentation'. A film-preview does two things: first of all, it gives you information, it tells you what is coming next; secondly, if it is a good preview, it makes you eager to see it by presenting the most exciting parts of the film. So you know what's coming and you are eager for it to arrive. The Resurrection is a preview: it gives us information and, if we will let it, it fills us with a joyful eagerness. It is God's way of informing us about what is coming next, for each of us and for his whole creation. It gives each of us the assurance that God has a future in store for us beyond death. Death, that terrible enemy of joy and love, will not consume us utterly. God has prepared for us a life beyond death of unimaginable glory.

But this hope is not just for us personally—it is for the *whole* of creation. *Everything* will have its fulfilment: the very sparrows that fall to the ground in the hard frost of winter will, in their way, participate in that transformed and glorified future. No drop of blood, no tear, no pang of sorrow or regret, will go unfulfilled—nothing, none of the small or great tragedies of man, will go unfulfilled or unexplained. And that is important, because there seems to be so much waste in creation, so much unexplained evil, such a suffocating weight of pain and torment. At times it fills us to the throat and we cry out to God for a sign: 'What does it mean, Lord? Why do you let it continue?' The Resurrection is God's answer to us. It is a trailer of his intentions. By this event he says: 'My children, you cannot know, as you are now, the reason for the misery that haunts my creation. You cannot understand the eternal battle that is waged between me and the mystery of evil. One day you shall, and all will be explained; but meanwhile trust me and accept this sign which I have raised up in history. By raising Jesus Christ from the brutal squalor of a criminal's death I have given you a preview, a foretaste, a glimpse into the final outcome of all things'. The Resurrection, then, like any good preview, gives us information: *it tells us what's coming.*

But it does more than that. It also tells us a little bit about what it will be like. It whets our appetite for God's great future. The best way to draw out the hints we are given in the Resurrection is to remember that God raised Jesus Christ, 'and him crucified', as Paul puts it. There was no wiping out of the crucifixion; no removing of the wounds; no plastic surgery done upon that tortured body. It was a *crucified* Christ who was raised, and his *very wounds* were radiant. In other words, the sufferings of Christ were not annulled or forgotten in the Resurrection; they were *glorified*, because they were an essential part of the new work of God in Christ. He was raised not *in spite* of suffering but *through* suffering. And this is the most releasing fact ever made known to man. It means that the very wounds that torture us, the pains of creation, the cries of children, the death of all our loves, are themselves to be *part* of our future glory. What God will do for us will not be in spite of suffering but through suffering. *He will make our wounds radiant!* We can only touch the fringe of this overpowering mystery, but it raises the problem of suffering to a new dimension. The Resurrection does not give us an answer to the problem of suffering; it gives suffering itself a new status; no longer a problem but, by some strange chemistry of the Spirit, a bearer of new life.

I have suffered very little in my life, but what little suffering

I have endured underlines this truth. God has frequently surprised me with new joy and love, and he has done this not as a reward for suffering but through suffering itself, suffering that I have frequently brought upon myself. The suffering becomes a bearer of mercy, a vehicle of joy. I cannot tell how God does this, but by some strategy of divine love he turns the very weapons of evil against itself. At God's final triumph, then, the very wounds of creation will be transformed and glorified, not forgotten.

In other words, the Resurrection is a great vision of the underlying union that binds together the conflict and duality of creation. God seems to be telling us that everything that happens to us and our world happens on two levels. There is the level that we see and feel, the level of worldly history, where men and women trudge through the gates of Auschwitz or are blown to bits in Belfast; the level where the young die of meaningless disease or the old lie crippled and twisted with arthritis. There is that level, and it accuses God. But there is another level which we cannot now see, where the same events are taken and worked upon by the patient love of God, and a slow and unconquerable glory is built from them. When St John talks about the crucifixion of Christ he uses the word *glorify*. The crucifixion of Christ is also *and at the same time* his glorification. Boris Pasternak makes the same truth general in some mysterious yet illuminating words: 'Everything that happens in the world takes place not only on the earth that buries the dead, but also in some other dimension which some call the Kingdom of God'.

This, then, is the vision which the Church exists to proclaim. We exist in the world as a sign of ultimate hope. We are obviously nothing in ourselves: 'less than the least of all men; the offscourings of the world';[8] but we point to a marvellous reality which is for all men. In the midst of the change and decay, the anguish and wistfulness of life, God sets up a sign which says: 'Nevertheless, there is meaning. In spite of it all, I reign, and even now I am bringing my kingdom to pass'. The Church is merely, yet wonderfully, a sign of the great 'Nevertheless!' of God.

Two things follow from this. First of all, the Church is not to be thought of as an ark of the saved floating upon the sea of the damned. It is a gathering of *some* men to whom God, in his mysterious providence, has given the knowledge of his saving purpose for *all* men. He has let us know and witness to 'the mystery of his purpose, the hidden plan he so kindly made known in Christ'.[9] And Paul goes on to say that God's plan was to bring 'everything together under Christ'. Not just those who have been sprinkled with the water of Baptism, but the whole creation which he loves with an everlasting and unconquerable love. So the Church is a representative community. It stands in history as a sign to all men of that great thing which God has prepared for them and is even now bringing to pass. We are like children who have seen the preview of next week's film: *we* know what's coming, but the show is for the whole neighbourhood. And that is a tremendous liberating insight. We do not have to feel threatened by or superior to those who have not yet become aware of the Reality which encompasses them. Faith is not a possession or a privilege; it is a way of seeing, a recognition; and what we see is for all men, even in this present time, though they know it not.

And this brings me to my last word. The real keynote of the Church's life should be joy—the joy that befits a community which has been let in on the secret of the ages. We are they who make eucharist in the midst of tragedy, because we have seen the glory that God is preparing for his wounded creation. Eucharistic joy! It is not, perhaps, the most conspicuous characteristic of contemporary Christianity, but it ought to be. Let me end by quoting some amazing words:

> Christian art is joyous because it is free, and it is free because of the fact of Christ's having died to redeem the world. One need not die in art nor save the world in it, those matters having been, so to speak, attended to. What is left? The blissful responsibility to enjoy the world.[10]

And these are not cheap words. They come from Osip Mandelstam, the greatest Russian poet of this century, who was hounded to death by Stalin in 1938. Christ has been raised from the dead, the first fruits of them that slept. What is left? The blissful responsibility to enjoy the world.

NOTES

CHAPTER 1

1 Some of which I have discussed in a previous Book: *Let God Arise*, Mowbrays (1972).
2 Dionysius the Areopagite: quoted in *The Spear of Gold*, p. 16. London, Burns Oates (1947), p. 16.
3 'The Mirror of Simple Souls': quoted in E. Underhill, *Mysticism*, London, Methuen (1967), p. 337.
4 Rebecca West: *The Birds Fall Down*, London, Macmillan (1966).
5 Charles Williams: *The Image of the City*, OUP (1970), p. xliii.

CHAPTER 2

1 W. H. Auden: '1st September 1939'.
2 The present population of the world is reckoned to be about 4,000 million.
3 Philip Larkin, *The Whitsun Wedding*.
4 Harry Golden, *Only in America*, New York: Permabooks (1959), p. 1.
5 Evelyn Underhill: *Letters*, London, Longmans, Green (1956), p. 301.
6 Gerard Manley Hopkins, 'Goldengrove'.
7 Graham Greene, *The Power and the Glory*.
8 Lewis Grassic Gibbon, *Sunset Song*, London, Longman (1971), p. 165.
9 Gerard Manley Hopkins, 'No Worst, There is None'.

CHAPTER 3

1 Theodore Roszak, *The Making of a Counter Culture*. London, Faber and Faber (1971), Doubleday, New York, (1969), pp. 237, 238.
2 Roszak, op.cit., p. 240.
3 E. L. Mascall, *Theology and the Future*. London, Darton Longman & Todd (1968), p. 63.
4 Joseph Heller, *Catch 22*, pp. 183–5 (American edition).

CHAPTER 4

1 In *Let God Arise* I have examined some of the consequences of this way of doing theology.
2 Roszak, op.cit., p. 211.

3 See especially chapter VII, pp. 205 ff., on which much of this chapter depends.
4 *Ibid.*, p. 215.
5 Cited by Roszak, pp. 278 ff.
6 *Ibid.*, p. 221.
7 *Ibid.*, p. 223.
8 *Ibid.*, pp. 226, 227.
9 *Ibid.*, p. 230.
10 *Ibid.*, pp. 231, 232.
11 *Ibid.*, p. 216.

CHAPTER 5

1 Roszak, op.cit., p. 224.
2 Evelyn Underhill, *Practical Mysticism*. London, J. M. Dent and Sons Ltd (1940), p. 4.

CHAPTER 6

1 Evelyn Underhill, *Mysticism*. London, Methuen and Co Ltd (1967), p. 76.
2 Op.cit., p. 94, cited from J. H. Leuba: *Revue Philosophique*, Juillet, 1922.
3 George Mackay Brown: *A Calendar of Love*. London: Hogarth Press (1967), pp. 32, 33.
4 Heb. 1.3. Phillips version.
5 John 7.46.
6 Mark 1.22.
7 1 John 1.1–4 in the Phillips version.

CHAPTER 7

1 Matt. 10.29.
2 Evelyn Underhill: *Letters*. London, Longmans, Green and Co. (1956), p. 301.
3 *Encyclopaedia Britannica*, 1962 edition: vol. 18, p. 720H. Article on Psychoses.
4 Rom. 7.24.
5 Acts 2.23.
6 John 1.13.
7 2 Cor. 5.19.
8 John 2.24.
9 St Augustine: *City of God*, XIV.15.
10 John 5.17.

11 Joachim Jeremias: *New Testament Theology* Vol. 1. London, SCM Press (1971), p. 119.
12 Luke 12.19.

CHAPTER 8

1 Joseph Klausner: *Jesus of Nazareth*, p. 368. Cited in Richard Niebuhr: *Christ and Culture*, New York, Harper Bros (1956), p. 3.
2 Romans 13.3, 4 (Moffat).
3 Neh. 4.17, 18. (R.V.)
4 Reinhold Niebuhr: *Man's Nature and His Communities*. New York, Charles Scribner (1965), p. 108.

CHAPTER 9

1 Dante, *Divine Comedy*, Paradiso, xxxiii.145.
2 Dorothy L. Sayers, *The Man Born to be King*. London, Victor Gollancz (1944), p. 310.

CHAPTER 10

1 Joachim Jeremias, *New Testament Theology*, Vol. 1. London, SCM Press (1971), p. 301.
2 W. S. Gilbert, *Iolanthe*.
3 Jeremias, op.cit., p. 301.
4 *Ibid.*, p. 303.
5 Jean Hering, *The First Epistle of Saint Paul to the Corinthians*. London, Epworth Press (1962), p. 160.
6 Jeremias, op.cit., p. 303.
7 *Ibid.*, p. 309.
8 1 Cor. 4.13.
9 Eph. 1.9.
10 Nadezhda Mandelstam, *Hope Against Hope*. London, Collins and Harvill Press (1971), p. x.